Coping with Loss
of Independence

Coping with Aging Series

Series Editors:
John C. Rosenbek, Ph.D.
Chief, Speech Pathology and Audiology Services
William S. Middleton Memorial Hospital
Madison, Wisconsin

Medical Editor:
Molly Carnes, M.D.
Department of Medicine and Institute on Aging
University of Wisconsin
Madison, Wisconsin

Associate Director for Clinical Services
Geriatric Research, Education and Clinical Center
William S. Middleton Memorial Hospital
Madison, Wisconsin

Published in Cooperation with
the National Council of Senior Citizens

Coping with Loss of Independence

Michael J. Siebers, M.D.
Gail Gunter-Hunt, M.S.W., A.C.S.W.
Jean Farrell-Holtan, O.T.R.

SINGULAR PUBLISHING GROUP, INC.
SAN DIEGO, CALIFORNIA

Published by Singular Publishing Group, Inc.
4284 41st Street
San Diego, California 92105

©1993 by Singular Publishing Group, Inc.

Typeset in 11/14 Times by So Cal Graphics
Printed in the United States of America by BookCrafters

Library of Congress Cataloging-in-Publication Data

Siebers, Michael J.
   Coping with loss of independence / by Michael J. Siebers,
  Gail Gunter-Hunt, Jean Farrell-Holtan.
      p.   cm.—(Coping with aging series)
    Includes index.
    ISBN 1-879105-60-8
     1. Aged—Health and hygiene.   2. Aged—Mental health.
  3. Autonomy in old age.   4. Aging—Psychological aspects.
  5. Aging —Social aspects.   I. Gunter-Hunt, Gail.
  II. Farrell-Holtan, Jean.   III. Title.   IV. Series.
  RA777.6.S58   1993
  155.67'2—dc20

                                     92-42197
                                       CIP
                                       r93

❖ Table of Contents

❖ Foreword

The books in the *Coping with Aging Series* are written for men and women coping with the challenges of aging, and for their families and other caregivers. The authors are all experienced practitioners; doctors, nurses, social workers, psychologists, pharmacists, nutritionists, audiologists, physical and occupational therapists, and speech-language pathologists.

The topics of individual volumes are as varied as are the challenges that aging may bring. These include: hearing loss, low vision, depression, sexual dysfunction, immobility, intellectual impairment, language impairment, speech impairment, swallowing impairment, death and dying, bowel and bladder incontinence, stress of caregiving, giving up independence, medications, and stroke. The volumes themselves, however, share common features. Foremost, they are practical, jargon-free, and responsible. Each contains professionally valid information translated into language people who are not health care providers can understand. Each contains useful advice and sections to help readers decide how they are doing and whether they need to do more, do less, or do something different. Each includes lists of services, suppliers, and additional readings. Each provides evidence that no single person need cope alone.

None of the volumes can substitute for appropriate professional health care. However, when combined with the care, instruction, and counseling that health care providers supply, they make coping with aging easier. America is greying at the same time its treasury is inadequate to meet its population's needs. Thus the *Coping with Aging Series* offers help for people who need and want to help themselves.

This volume, *Coping with Loss of Independence*, is written by professionals with knowledge of the medical, social, and environmental needs of adults as they age. Each author has at least ten years of experience working in a professional capacity with older adults. If you have questions about medical problems or the standards of preventive health care, this book will help. If you are having problems related to meal preparation, bathing, maintaining home safety or problems related to other activities of daily living, this book can help. If you are thinking of moving to a nursing home or elsewhere in your community, this book can help. If you have questions about guardianships or money issues of importance to the older adult, this book can help. This book covers many issues related to the loss of independence in words you can understand. No person with loss of independence should feel without help to cope with their problems.

John C. Rosenbek, Ph.D.
Series Editor

Molly Carnes, M.D.
Medical Editor

❖ Preface

Throughout the life span, great value is placed on achieving and maintaining independence. The issues that will affect your independence or the independence of someone you are caring for are complex and sometimes beyond your control. You undoubtedly will need to adapt to the changes in your life brought on by your health status, your housing arrangements, the presence of a caregiver, and the availability of community services. Your ability to make these adaptations will decrease your risk for losing some parts of your independence as you age.

Coping with Loss of Independence can help you address these issues head-on! It provides information to help you understand the important elements of independent functioning and how to access resources to maintain independence. It is written in lay language, free of medical jargon, and it is full of helpful facts and information.

The first chapter provides a basic recipe for independence. Subsequent chapters give you tips on selecting a doctor and preventing illness when you can. If you do become ill, the chapter on "Regaining Function After Illness or Hospitalization" can help you learn how to become an active participant in your own recovery. Basic health issues such as sadness, depression, arthritis, falls, safety, and the ability to provide self-care are discussed, because you may at some time face some of these problems.

Coping with Loss of Independence concludes with chapters that focus on areas of independence such as locating appropriate housing, driving or arranging transportation, managing finances, and coordinating legal arrangements. Then, an Appendix of Resource Agencies and Advocacy Groups is included for further information on particular topics.

❖ Acknowledgments

We acknowledge the help and support of the series editors. We also thank the Medical Media Departments at the Wm. S. Middleton Memorial Veterans Hospital and University of Wisconsin Hospital and Clinics for help with drawings and photographs. We thank the University of Wisconsin Medical School Department of Medicine Secretarial Center for help with manuscript preparation. We wish to thank Dr. Michael Hunt for reviewing Chapter 10, Ms. Paulette Siebers for reviewing Chapter 13, Mr. Paul Holtan for reviewing Chapters 4 and 8, and Dr. Krishna Dasgupta for reviewing Chapter 6. We acknowledge the University of Wisconsin Photographic Media Center for taking the photographs used in this book. We also acknowledge the ongoing support of the University of Wisconsin Department of Medicine and the Geriatric Research, Education and Clinical Center (GRECC) at the Wm. S. Middleton Memorial Veterans Hospital. Of course, any defects or errors in the book are the responsibility of the authors. This book was written to explore and advise on issues related to maintaining independence and coping with loss of independence. No reader should ever apply or interpret his or her own situation without the help of professionals who know the facts, the interests, and the goals being pursued.

Nothing is inherently and invincibly young except the spirit.

George Santayana

❖ Dedication

This book is dedicated to our families: Paulette, Nicholas, and Ruth; Mike, Sarah, and Lois; and Paul and Carl. We also dedicate the book to our colleagues and especially to the older adults whom we care for and who have helped us learn.

Chapter 1

A Recipe for Independence

Independence is important and cherished. Disease and advanced age can lead to loss of independence. The recipe for maintaining independence in the face of disease and aging has several ingredients all required in a unique blend to meet your difficulties. In this chapter each of these ingredients is described.

What is Function?

Functional ability is the ability to carry out the daily tasks necessary to live. Many of the changes that accompany aging or disease make it difficult for people to be independent in performing these tasks. These tasks, called "activities of daily living" or "ADLs," are divided into basic ADLs and instrumental ADLs.

Basic ADLs necessary for survival include eating, bathing, getting in and out of bed, getting around inside and outside the home, getting dressed, and going to the bathroom. Instrumental ADLs are more complex tasks that a person must accomplish to manage safely for any length of time in a house or apartment; these tasks include preparing meals, buying groceries, doing laundry, using leisure time, managing money, using the telephone, doing housework, and managing medications (see the photograph on p. 3). Basic ADLs and instrumental ADLs are discussed at length in Chapter 4. The performance of ADLs is referred to as "function" or "functional ability." Individuals who require help with ADLs are often referred to as being "functionally impaired."

Shopping and leisure activities are two of the instrumental activities of daily living.

Why Do People Need Help with ADLs?

Assistance with ADLs is necessary for two broad categories of disability. The first category is physical frailty. The physically frail may be unable to perform their ADLs because of physical limitations. For example, it may be difficult to bathe or dress because of arthritis. The second category is memory or cognitive impairment. People with memory or cognitive impairment may forget how to perform ADLs or be unaware that any help is needed. Usually, physical frailty or memory impairment result from disease; however, for adults over 80 years old, aging itself may play a role. For the memory-impaired or physically frail adult, supervision may be needed in addition to or instead of hands-on assistance with ADLs.

How Common is Functional Impairment?

Functional impairment is common in older adults. By the time people are over age 85, one-third of those living in the community will require assistance with some or all ADLs. People living in nursing homes have an even greater need for assistance with ADLs. Sometimes the need for assistance is temporary, such as after a heart attack or surgery. Sometimes the need for assistance is permanent, such as in the person with severe arthritis or marked memory and judgment impairment.

Who Helps Out When Function is Impaired?

People who provide assistance with ADLs are called caregivers. A large voluntary caregiver system in the United States is centered around the family. On average, family members of people with functional impairment spend 1 to 4 years providing care 365 days a year with no financial reimbursement. The most likely family member to act as a caregiver is the wife, followed by daughters, husbands, and sons. Caregiving includes tasks such as meal preparation, providing transportation, helping with the bills, and offering emotional support.

Caregiving by the family can be augmented by personal attendants hired either privately or through an agency. Personal care attendants are discussed further in Chapters 4 and 10. The types of help personal attendants may provide include:

- Bathing

- Dressing

- Getting in and out of bed

- Care of teeth, mouth, dentures, and hair

- Assistance with mobility

- Skin care, including nails

- Laundry

- Toileting

- Meal preparation

Some of these services also may be obtained through day care programs, meal sites, visiting nurse services, or volunteer organizations. When people are quite functionally impaired or have no caregiver, nursing home care may be needed (see Chapter 11).

Caregivers become more important as people become more impaired. In general, the stronger the caregiver support network the longer one can live at home. Conversely a weak caregiving system may result in premature admission to a nursing home. Of course, living at home for a longer time would be preferable for most persons and is usually less expensive. An integral part of "a comprehensive geriatric assessment" recommended for older adults at risk of losing independence involves identifying caregivers and nurturing them in this role.

The Geriatric Assessment Team: A New State of the Art

The needs of the older adult are often complex. A comprehensive geriatric assessment by a team of health care professionals may best be suited to the individual over 75 years of age or the frail person with multiple problems. This assessment may be helpful when the physician working alone is unable to meet particular needs or address concerns not related to a specific medical problem. Many medical groups and community hospitals have the resources for a geriatric assessment. Ask your physician if geriatric assessment or consultation is available in your community or contact the closest medical center.

The team involved in the assessment typically is composed of a diverse group of professionals interested in and committed to the study of aging (called gerontology) and the health care of older adults (called geriatrics). Professional disciplines of assessment team members vary, but social work, nursing, and medicine are essential. Physical and occupational therapy, psychiatry, neurology, audiology, pharmacy, dietary services, and others also may be included or available by consultation. This assessment may be undertaken in the home, clinic, or hospital settings.

What to Expect From an Assessment

The goals of a comprehensive geriatric assessment include:

• making sure medical diagnoses are correct

- working with you and your family to develop a practical plan for care

- helping adapt the environment, if necessary, to promote function

- providing or arranging for necessary services in the home.

A geriatric assessment will include evaluation of performance of ADLs, and the emphasis of recommended interventions is usually on promoting and maintaining function. A geriatric assessment does not overlook medical problems, but it is not limited to them.

Studies completed to date on the comprehensive geriatric assessment suggest that when it is properly implemented and coupled with appropriate ongoing care, a better outcome can result for many older adults than what usually results from traditional care. The most dramatic improvement is lower death rates in older adults who undergo assessment. If this sounds too good to be true, note that careful selection of older people for this service is very important. If you are very limited functionally or very debilitated, you may not benefit from a geriatric assessment. People with mild to moderate impairments appear to derive the most benefit. Note also that not all insurance sources will reimburse for this assessment.

Other Resources for Help

If you are having difficulty in everyday tasks or caregiving for someone who is functionally impaired, a "case manager"

might be helpful. Case management is a service organized to evaluate needs and obtain services for those needs. Case management provides advocacy for the functionally impaired. The case manager may work closely with a physician in settings such as a geriatric assessment clinic, a stroke clinic, or a rehabilitation medicine program. Case managers also may be available privately, although most insurance will not reimburse for case management services. Case management skills also may be available through state, county, or municipal organizations. For example, a visiting nurse or community social worker may act as a case manager. Hospice programs designed for the terminally ill have a strong case management style. Service organizations or health care groups, such as the Alzheimer's Association, may be able to offer or direct you to some case management help (see Appendix).

Summary

Independence in ADLs is the goal. In many respects you define your own independence and how to achieve it. To maintain independence in the face of disease or aging, you must identify the problems and develop a recipe, a plan, a strategy, to solve those problems. You may not be able to design this strategy without professional help. You may need help from a caregiver or other support people to implement the plan. With aid and support, independence is possible even when you are facing illness and aging.

References

Some of the information in this chapter was adapted from the following sources:

Baum, C. M. (1991). Addressing the needs of the cognitively impaired elderly from a family policy perspective. *American Journal of Occupational Therapy, 45,* 594–606.

Keddie, K.M.G. (1978). *Action with the elderly: A handbook for relatives and friends.* Oxford: Pergamon Press.

Levy, M. T. (1991). *Parenting mom and dad.* New York: Prentice-Hall.

National Institutes of Health. (1987, October19–21). Geriatric assessment methods for clinical decisionmaking. *Consensus Development Conference Statement, 6,* 13.

Chapter 2

Choosing a Doctor

With age, you are more likely to develop several medical problems. The maze of health care professionals available can be overwhelming. This chapter will define some of the types of physicians who provide care, describe the different settings in which physicians may practice, describe some of the nonphysician health care professionals who may be involved in your care, and provide a list of questions you may want to ask your physician.

Physicians Who Offer Primary Care

In general, it is beneficial to have a physician who manages your overall health care or a "primary care physician." A primary care physician should see you on a regular basis, know you well, and coordinate your medical care through the maze of medical and surgical specialists. The primary care doctor also offers patient education and preventive health care (see Chapter 3).

It is recommended that even healthy older adults visit their doctor every 2 years between the ages of 65 and 74 and every year after age 75. Individuals with illness may need to be seen more often. Family Practitioners, General Practitioners, Internists, and sometimes Geriatricians most often serve as primary care physicians. General Surgeons, Gynecologists, or other subspecialists serve as primary care physicians for some people, but may not be ideal for older adults. The amount and type of training for the primary care physicians is as follows:

- *Family Practitioner*: A physician who provides care for individuals of all ages. A Family Practitioner must have 3 years of training (residency) beyond medical school to take a national examination and must pass that examination to be board certified. Many groups of health care professionals, physicians, and other providers, have specialty boards that set requirements for certification.

• *General Internist*: A physician who provides primary care for adults and who sometimes serves as a consultant to other physicians. A General Internist must have 3 years of residency beyond medical school to take a national examination and pass that examination to be board certified. This physician may become a subspecialist by completing a fellowship in such areas as cardiology (heart), pulmonary medicine (lung), rheumatology (joints), nephrology (kidneys), or geriatrics (aging).

• *General Practitioner (the "GP")*: A physician who has completed medical school. The amount of training a General Practitioner is required to have beyond medical school varies from state to state; usually, it is a 1-year internship.

• *Geriatrician*: An Internist or Family Practitioner with special training in the problems of older adults, usually obtained by training for 2 years beyond residency in a fellowship. Since 1988, a national examination has been available, and physicians who pass this examination are awarded a certificate of added qualification in geriatric medicine. A Geriatrician may be part of a geriatric assessment team (see Chapter 1).

Residency and fellowship programs can be based in university hospitals or hospitals that are closely affiliated with universities or medical schools, or they can be based in community hospitals. Physicians must have a license for the state in which they practice medicine.

Questions to Ask
When Looking for a Doctor

Look for a physician until you find one suited to your needs. Your physician should listen to you, and you should feel comfortable expressing yourself. Good medicine should not be a bitter pill. Think of your first visit to a new physician as a job interview for the doctor. Don't be afraid to ask a doctor about his or her philosophy of patient care. If you have areas of special concern, get the answers regarding those areas. Don't be afraid to ask your doctors what kind of training they have had.

If you feel you aren't receiving good care, try a different doctor. Use the Yellow Pages; ask your friends about their doctors; or call the Medical Society in your community. Cities, counties, and states all have Medical Societies of physicians working in the community. Medical Societies have a telephone number and address in the local phone book; usually the state society is located in the state capital. It is important to trust your doctor. Together, you and your doctor will be making important decisions that will affect your life.

If you do see a new doctor, be sure to bring copies of your medical records with you. This will save time and expense, because the old records can be reviewed when you first meet a new physician and used immediately to assess your needs. It can save extra visits to the physician's office. All physicians and hospitals have "Release of Medical Information Forms" that legally allow records to be sent to a new doctor or provided directly to you. You should not be worried that you will offend your doctor. This is a common practice.

Suggested questions to ask when choosing a doctor are:

1. Did you complete a residency? What kind? Are you Board Certified?

2. Are you in private practice or do you work for a clinic, hospital, or health maintenance organization?

3. If you are in a group practice or clinic, are the other physicians in your specialty or different specialties?

4. Are you affiliated with a university or medical school? Will I be seen by physicians in training?

5. Where do I go if I need to have blood tests or X-rays?

6. What should I do if I get sick on a weekend or after hours?

7. What hospital do you admit your patients to?

8. What doctor will take care of me if I am admitted to the hospital?

9. Do you have other health care professionals such as a social worker or nurse practitioner available in a clinic or by referral?

10. Do you take Medicare assignment?

11. Will you visit me in my home if I cannot make it to the clinic?

12. If I need to go to a nursing home, will you continue to be my doctor?

13. Where do you send patients who need consultation?

If you are uncomfortable asking these questions yourself, take this book with you and read the questions to the doctor.

Where Will You Go to See Your Doctor?

Physicians practice in a variety of different settings. They may practice alone as solo practitioners, in a group or clinic with other physicians of the same specialty, in a group or clinic with other physicians of different specialties, or in a hospital that serves as a training site for nurses, other health care providers, or physicians. Each type of practice has advantages and disadvantages. Ideally, you can pick the setting in which you are most comfortable. For example, university-affiliated clinics may have access to a broader range of consultants than other types of practice, but you may have to be seen by physicians-in-training as well as your doctor. Also, you should be aware that most doctors in university settings have many other duties beside patient care and may be less available to you.

While your primary care physician can manage most of your medical problems, you may periodically need to be referred to specialists. A list of medical and surgical specialists are given in the chart on page 18. For example, your doctor may refer you to an ophthalmologist for cataracts, to a neurologist for stroke or Parkinson's disease, or to a rheumatologist for arthritis. The specialist usually sends a report back to your primary care physician. You may see the specialist once or several times.

Nonphysician Health Care Professionals Who May Participate in Your Care

Most clinics that specialize in providing care to older adults will have a social worker, nurse, nurse practitioner, or other health care professionals either working in the clinic or readily accessible by consultation. The services of these professionals can be invaluable in providing care to someone who is functionally impaired.

Some of these professionals are:

- *Nurse Practitioner:* A nurse who has had advanced nursing, usually 2 years in a master's program beyond nursing school. Nurse practitioner skills include physical examination, medication use and action, and patient education and health maintenance.

- *Social Worker:* A person with a minimum of a bachelor's degree in social work. Many social workers choose advanced training in a 2-year master's degree program. They provide counseling for personal or family problems, including adjustment to illness, disability, bereavement, caregiver stress, adjustment to retirement, marital or family conflict, and financial stress.

Specialty Doctors
Often Seen by Older Adults

Doctor's Title	Area of Specialization
Medical	
Nephrologist	Urine and kidney problems
Gastroenterologist	Stomach, liver, and colon
Rheumatologist	Joints and bones
Hematologist	Blood and lymph system
Oncologist	Tumors and cancer
Endocrinologist	Diabetes, thyroid disorders, and metabolism
Psychiatrist	Psychological or behavioral problems
Neurologist	Brain and nerves
Pulmonologist	Lungs, often sleep disorders
Cardiologist	Heart, heart valves, and blood vessels
Surgical	
Urologist	Operates on kidneys, bladder, prostate and male sex organs
Gynecologist	Female sex organs
General Surgeon	Operates on intestines, hernias, thyroid gland, gallbladder, and other areas of the abdomen
Orthopedist	Operates on bone and joints
Otolaryngologist	Ears, nose, and throat
Ophthalmologist	Eyes
Cardiovascular Surgeon	Operates on heart and blood vessels
Podiatrist	Feet

They also help individuals or families with case management, health care planning, discharge planning from hospitals or nursing homes, and coordinate referrals to appropriate community agencies. Social workers are licensed or certified.

- *Physician Assistant:* An individual who has completed an approved Physician Assistant Program. Physician assistants help physicians with medical procedures, routine care, or emergency visits as arranged between the physician and the assistant.

- *Occupational Therapist (OT):* A person graduated from a 4-year professional program with a focus on working with physical and psychological disabilities. Many have advanced master's training. OTs make adaptive home equipment and counsel on a balance of self-care, work, rest, and play to maintain and increase function. They must pass a national examination to become registered.

- *Physical Therapist (PT):* A person graduated from a 4-year professional program with a focus on improving strength, motion, and coordination. After course work, PTs complete affiliations or internships for 3 months. PTs provide gait training, muscle strengthening, and aides to walking. PTs are licensed (see Chapter 8).

- *Dietician:* An individual with a bachelor's degree in nutrition or dietetics. They complete a 6- to 12-month internship, are registered by a national board examination, and may take advanced training for a master's degree. Dieticians assess nutritional state and dietary needs.

- *Pharmacist:* A person who has graduated from a 5-year pharmacy school. They complete a 1-year internship and are licensed by the state and a national association. Pharmacists dispense medicine and educate patients about medication use and interactions.

This review covers many, but not all, of the types of non-physician health care providers who can assess and assist you.

Summary

There are many types of physicians and other health care providers. To get the best health care, find a competent doctor—one you trust. Good medical care will help to soften the difficulties and suffering that aging and illness can impose. Services from health care professionals other than the physician should be available through your physician. Altogether, these services can help keep you independent.

Chapter 3

Preventing Illness and Retaining Functional Ability

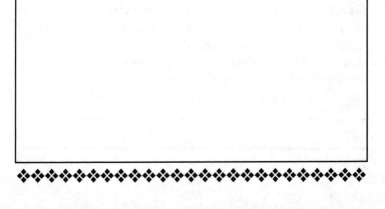

Although there are people in their 80s who continue to run marathons, aging is associated with many physical changes that can make it more difficult to perform the activities of daily living described in Chapters 1 and 4. The processes of aging can't be prevented. Neither can the onset of many diseases. There are, however, a number of decisions you can make about your lifestyle that can slow the loss of function due to aging and prevent some diseases. Outlined in the chart below are the lifestyle choices that help individuals maintain health and function. These lifestyle choices are discussed in this chapter.

Don't Smoke

Smoking is harmful to health at any age. It causes irreversible loss of lung function, leads to heart disease, and is a major risk factor for cancer. If you quit smoking at

Lifestyle Changes That
Slow Aging or Prevent Disease

Don't smoke
Exercise regularly
Eat well
Get adequate rest
Have regular history and physical examinations with physician
Have your hearing, vision and functional ability assessed regularly
Get your blood pressure checked
Have regular earwax and toenail care if needed
Consider screening tests for disease
Get your vaccinations up-to-date

30, it's good for you. If you quit smoking at 90, it's still good for you. Quit smoking, or don't start. If you can't stop, at least try to smoke less. Some clinics or hospitals have programs designed to help smokers stop smoking. Ask your doctor. Put the money aside you save from not smoking and buy yourself a present. You deserve it.

Exercise Regularly

Regular exercise is recommended throughout life. Exercise can improve endurance, strength, and flexibility. It can also improve your sense of well-being, decrease pain, and improve the quality of your life.

In general, aerobics-type classes geared toward younger participants should be avoided unless you have gradually worked your way up to this type of rigorous exercise. Exercise classes geared toward older adults are now widely available. Call your local Senior Center, YMCA/YWCA, or health club and ask. To make an exercise program successful, it should be fun. Exercise with a friend or to music. Vary the routine from day to day, but try to exercise on a regular basis. Write to the American Physical Therapy Association at 1111 North Fairfax Street, Alexandria, VA 22314 for more information on exercise programs.

Consult with a Physician or Physical Therapist

If you are undertaking a new exercise program regardless of how rigorous and if you have some health problems, check with your doctor or physical therapist first. Your exercise program should be tailored to your needs and limitations. For example, bicycle riding in general is better for people with knee problems, but not as good for those with hip problems. Arthritis in the neck is present in almost everyone by age 70 or 80. So avoid forcing your neck into a position that hurts or holding your neck in an awkward position. Either of these can make the arthritis flare up or pinch nerves or blood vessels in your neck. See Chapter 7 for more information on joint protection. If you have pain with any exercise, limit that type of exercise and consult with your physician or physical therapist.

Elements of a Good Exercise Program

There are four components to an exercise program: stretching, warm-up, exercising, and cool-down.

Stretching

Stretching has several goals. It can be used after an injury for rehabilitation of the muscle, ligaments (structures that hold bones together), or tendons (structures that hold bone to muscle). Stretching is a good form of preconditioning and loosening the muscles and skeletal system for more vigorous activity. It will also reduce the risk of injury from exercise.

Stretching should be done in a slow and methodical fashion without bouncing. Each stretching position should be held for 15 to 45 seconds. You should be able to feel the muscle being stretched, and it should feel good when you stop.

The illustrations on pages 26–28 demonstrate a group of stretching and warm-up exercises that may be beneficial for you. The first illustration (p. 26) demonstrates a set of neck stretches. They can be done from a sitting or standing position. Start with your head, neck, and shoulders upright. First, let your head fall back producing a stretch on the front of your neck for 20 seconds. Second, let your head drop slowly forward to allow the weight of your head to stretch the muscles of the back of your neck for 20 seconds. Next, drop your ear toward your shoulder. The stretch is felt in the opposite side of the neck. Do this stretch to the right and left holding each position for 20 seconds. Finally, rotate your chin toward your shoulder, again both right and left, and hold for 20 seconds. When you stretch your neck muscles, you should not feel like you are forcing your neck into an extreme position and your neck should not hurt.

The second illustration (p. 27) demonstrates two stretches for your back and legs. Sit on the floor with legs apart but in a comfortable position. First, reach out between your feet, bending your back while keeping your neck and shoulders straight. Then, reach out sequentially to both feet with one arm on either side of your legs. Hold each of these stretches for 30 to 45 seconds. You will feel the muscles in your back, groin, and legs stretching. You may not be able to reach all the way to your foot.

The next stretches are also done while on the floor. You will want a little padding on the floor for the stretches in the third illustration (p. 28). While lying on your back, gently pull one knee to your chest. Keep your lower back flat. Hold the position for 20 seconds, then repeat with

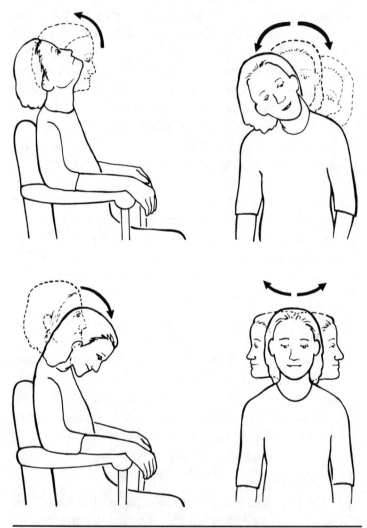

Neck stretches. (Modified from *Exercises for Health*, 1986, by John R. Sallade with permission of the American Physical Therapy Association.)

Back, groin, and leg stretches. (Modified from *Exercises for Health,* 1986, by John R. Sallade with permission of the American Physical Therapy Association.)

the other knee. Three to five repetitions should produce a mild stretch in the lower back. As you limber up, pull up both knees together for 15 to 30 seconds. Lie on your back to relax for a minute. While lying down, do an elongation stretch by extending your arms over your head and straightening your legs out for 10 seconds as if you're being pulled on a rack. When doing the elongation stretch, think of yourself as Superman or Superwoman flying upside down on your back. Then roll over and repeat the stretch for 10 seconds flying on your stomach.

Back and leg stretches. (Modified from *Exercises for Health*, 1986, by John R. Sallade with permission of the American Physical Therapy Association.)

The fourth illustration (p. 30) demonstrates two stretches for your back and stomach muscles done from a hand-knee position. Let your back sag like a tired horse, and tighten the lower back muscles. Hold this position for 10 seconds, then relax, then arch your back up. When you arch your back, you'll tighten stomach muscles and stretch the lower back.

Bob Anderson has written a book entitled *Stretching* (see Further Readings section), which is an excellent guide. Each stretch program needs to be individualized to some extent depending on exercises to be undertaken and your ability. Although stretching takes time, it leads to major improvements in well-being, and its value should not be shortchanged.

Warm-Ups

Warm-ups follow stretching and involve about 5 minutes of activity at a speed between stretching and full exercise. This could be a walk around the block or riding a stationary bike at a slow speed.

The fifth illustration (p. 31) demonstrates a good warm-up for the arms and shoulders. Start with your arms stretched out from the sides of your body and move them in small circles. Make progressively larger circles and raise your arms above your head. Your heart rate will increase, and your arms will become tired. Stop when you feel burning in your arms or shoulders. Work up to a minute. The burning sensation in your muscle is a result of muscle use and fatigue. It is normal during exercise and goes away when you rest.

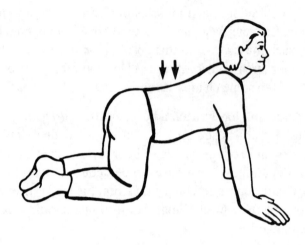

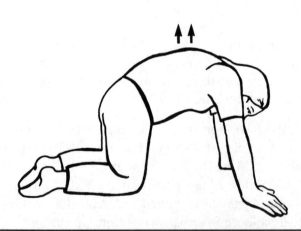

Back and abdomen stretches. (Modified from *Exercises for Health*, 1986, by John R. Sallade with permission of the American Physical Therapy Association.)

Arm and shoulder warm-ups. (Modified from *Exercises for Health*, 1986, by John R. Sallade with permission of the American Physical Therapy Association.)

The sixth illustration (p. 33) demonstrates back and side leg lifts done while leaning on the back of a chair. Slowly raise your leg to the side or the back. If you can, repeat each leg lift up to 10 times or to the point of fatigue when you feel a burning in the buttock or hips.

The seventh illustration (p. 34) demonstrates two warm-up exercises for the thigh and calf. The drawing in the upper panel demonstrates how to sit on and stand up from a chair without using your arms. Keep your back straight and go up and down slowly so you feel the thigh and buttock muscles stretch. This exercise could be done to tolerance or up to 10 times. The drawing in the lower panel demonstrates a good exercise for your calf and ankle. While sitting down, pump your foot up and down in rapid alternation for 20 to 30 seconds. Exercise to the calf and foot is important for helping to maintain balance while walking.

Warm-ups help to limber you prior to greater exertion. Therefore, you should spend at least 10 minutes on stretching and warm-up exercises.

Exercise

It is important to move every one of your joints through its full range of motion or as far through the range as you can for joint, bone, and muscle fitness at least once a day. In addition, the exercise portion of your workout should improve your cardiovascular (heart and blood vessel) conditioning. To ensure heart or cardiovascular fitness your exercise should last at least 20 minutes, increase your heart rate slightly (approximately 20 percent), and cause you to break into a mild sweat. Many exercise pro-

**Leg and hip warm-ups. (Modified from *Exercises for
Health*, 1986, by John R. Sallade with permission of
the American Physical Therapy Association.)**

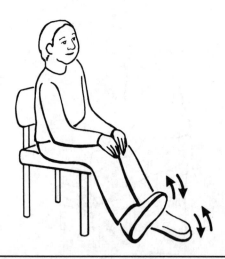

Upper panel, leg and buttock warm-up; lower panel, calf and ankle warm-up. (Modified from *Exercises for Health*, 1986, by John R. Sallade with permission of the American Physical Therapy Association.)

grams involve calisthenics or other aerobic exercises. However, bowling, tennis, golf, swimming, bicycling, and walking (to name a few) are all excellent exercise activities. In *Exercise for Health*, John R. Sallade outlines several progressive exercise programs you may find useful (see Further Readings). With practice, your endurance will improve and perhaps your skill also. As you improve, you may be able to add more strenuous or complex exercises to increase your level of enjoyment.

Walking

Walking, the exercise preferred by the authors, provides heel-strike activity or weight-bearing activity that is important to prevent osteoporosis. Walking is quite versatile. It can be done with a group or by yourself. You can walk in a shopping mall if the weather is bad or outdoors to enjoy fine weather and scenery. As you gain strength and endurance, you can increase the speed or length of time you walk to increase heart and lung conditioning. The risk of injury from walking is quite small compared to other exercise activities.

Walking is an excellent exercise even if done slowly. Wear something white or brightly colored if you walk at night so you can be seen. Comfortable, supportive footwear is also important, particularly if you have foot, knee, or hip problems; but no high-tech, expensive equipment is required for walking.

Cool-Down

After exercise, you need a cool-down period of 5 to 10 minutes doing activities similar to your warm-up and stretching. Walking at a slower rate than during exercise is an excellent cool-down activity. You may focus your stretching during cool-down on parts of your body that feel stiff or that need more protection because of arthritis or injury.

Eat Well

Diet is important for health. Body weight increases up to 40–50 years of age then remains stable for 15–20 years; after this, it declines slowly even if people eat wisely. The decline in weight after age 65 means that older adults don't need to eat as much food.

However, the quality of the diet is still important and should include protein, calories, vitamins, and minerals. The "tea-and-toast diet" is lacking in vitamins and protein. Processed meats are less expensive and easier to chew and prepare, but may be a poor source of protein and are also high in sodium (salt). Salt is not inherently bad for you but should be avoided if you have fluid retention, high blood pressure (hypertension), or kidney disease. The potassium content of processed foods is also lower. Potassium is an important element in your diet for many metabolic processes of your body. Processed foods such as toaster pastries, TV dinners, packaged cold cuts, and canned vegetables are typically low in fiber and often high in sugar. All of these changes in processed foods make them less healthy foods.

Fiber is particularly important in your diet. Dietary fiber is in fruits, vegetables, nuts, grains, and legumes (beans and peas). Fiber is also called roughage and represents a portion of food your body does not digest. A fiber-rich diet may lower your risk for colon cancer, reduce episodes of constipation, help with weight reduction, and reduce your serum cholesterol level. Bran is a good source of fiber. You can buy bran at the grocery store and sprinkle it on a variety of other foods. Other practical ways to increase the fiber in your diet include:

- eat more fruits and vegetables

- eat less processed foods

- eat more cereal and grain, for example, try whole wheat pasta, brown rice, or bran muffins

- choose cereals or breads that have more fiber (food labels will give you comparisons)

- try beans and peas in soups, salads, or casseroles

If you are changing from a low- to a high-fiber diet, do so gradually so your digestive system can adjust. Your bowel movements will increase in size and become softer. You may feel more bloated at first. To reduce the gas-producing effects of dried beans and peas, boil them for 2 minutes then soak them for 4 to 5 hours before cooking them in fresh water.

Some older adults weigh more than their ideal body weight and need dietary or calorie restrictions to lose weight. Weight loss can lead to improvement in arthritic pain in the lower back, hips, and knees. It can also result in better control of diabetes and hypertension. If your cholesterol level is high, a change in your diet might be helpful. Consult a physician or dietitian about weight-loss programs for specific diseases. Skipping second helpings, snacks and desserts is a good way to prevent weight gain. Unexplained or unwanted weight loss is discussed in Chapter 5.

Get Adequate Rest

Adequate sleep is important to maintain health. Without a good night's rest you may be fatigued the following day. Sleeping poorly night after night will leave you psychologically and physically depleted. The amount of sleep required at night does decline with advancing age. Some people need as few as 5 or 6 hours a night. If you require 6 hours of sleep and go to bed at 9:00 p.m., you will awake at 3:00 a.m. ready to shake, rattle, and roll! The best remedy for this is a later bedtime, not a sleeping pill. Another change in sleep pattern that occurs with age is an increase in brief awakenings during the night. These brief awakenings generally do not interfere with your sense of feeling rested when you arise in the morning.

Promoting Good Sleep

One of the best ways to ensure a good night's sleep is to be active during the day. Avoid long or multiple naps during the day or you won't be tired at night. Some people will retire early because of boredom, fear of being alone, or of having intruders at night. Sometimes, going to bed early can be an avoidance behavior to escape something unpleasant. If you can't fall asleep, get up and do something for a while. If you're in bed every night for 20 minutes, or longer, before falling asleep, this will become a routine. If you have trouble sleeping, use your bed only for sleeping—not reading, working, or watching TV. It's helpful to have your bed associated only with sleep. Try to establish a tranquil bedtime routine, for example, quiet reading and a glass of milk, or a soothing bath, that's conducive to sleep. Don't take stimulants like caffeine or tobacco before bedtime. Alcohol is also a stimulant and should not be taken immediately before bed. Sleeping pills disrupt the normal pattern of sleep and lead to poor sleep quality if used for longer than a few days. Nonetheless, they are among the most commonly (and probably the most incorrectly) prescribed medications.

Difficulty sleeping can be an indication of a health problem. You may awaken at night to pass urine because of prostate, bladder, or heart problems. This can also occur with water pill (diuretic) medications taken late in the day. Awakening with chest pain or trouble breathing could indicate anxiety, heart or lung disease, arthritis, or stomach problems. Trouble falling asleep or awakening in the early morning can occur from depression. If you are having persistent trouble sleeping, talk to your doctor.

Yearly History and Physical Examination

Between age 65 to 75 a history and physical exam is recommended every other year and over age 75 every year.

The history and physical examination generally includes an assessment of vision and hearing and should assess functional abilities for older adults (see Chapter 1). Over-the-counter and prescription medications should also be reviewed. Weight, height, and blood pressure are also recorded during the examination. High blood pressure can lead to stroke or heart problems. Most people with high blood pressure feel perfectly well. High blood pressure is readily treated, so your blood pressure should be checked regularly. A major task force on health screening recommends an in-home evaluation for the "progressive incapacity of aging" for individuals greater than 74 years old. A study done in Denmark demonstrated that when people over 74 years of age were called or visited in their homes every 3 months there were fewer hospitalizations, fewer deaths, and less money spent than among people who did not have this service.

Screening

Some diseases can be detected and treated early, before your health is impaired. Looking for these conditions is called "screening." Although there is still debate among physicians on many issues in screening, general agreement exists that screening and early treatment are beneficial for conditions listed in the chart on page 41. These recommendations are for otherwise healthy individuals who have no symptoms of illness. Whenever you develop *any* new symptom, you should check with your doctor.

Breast, prostate, and colon cancer are common in older adults, and early discovery can lead to a cure. Breast

Screen Tests Recommended, Frequency of Testing, and Diseases Screened for in Adults Over 65 Years of Age

Recommended Test	Frequency of Testing	Disease
History and physical exam from physician	Yearly (over age 75) or every 2 years (ages 65 to 75)	General well-being
Height and weight	Every 2 years	General well-being
Breast exam for women	Yearly	Breast cancer
Blood pressure measurement	Every visit	Hypertension
Pap smear for women	Every 1 to 3 years; may stop if consistently normal for 3 years	Cervical cancer
Mammogram for women	Every 1 to 2 years from 60 to 75, then discuss with your doctor	Breast cancer
Occult blood testing in bowel movements	Yearly	Colon cancer
Serum cholesterol measurement	Every 3 to 5 years	Hyperlipidemia
Thyroid function tests	Every 3 to 5 years	Thyroid disease

examination and mammography can detect breast cancer early. Checking the bowel movement with a chemical test for a small amount of blood ("occult blood") can detect colon cancer early. There is still no good screening procedure for prostate cancer, and the routine use of a blood test for prostate cancer (PSA or "prostate specific antigen") is controversial.

Toenails and Ears are Important

Other areas of prevention to consider are (1) regular toenail care to prevent painful feet and difficulty walking and (2) regular removal of wax from your ears to prevent unnecessary loss of hearing.

If you can't cut your own toenails because you can't see, because you get dizzy when you bend over, or because they're very thick, ask for help. Long toenails can interfere with balance or lead to infection. Routine nail care may be available through your medical clinic. Some local agencies offer foot clinics for older adults at a low price. Podiatrists are practitioners who specialize in diseases of the foot. You may get routine nail care through some podiatric offices. For earwax removal, you can buy a kit at most drug stores that comes with a bulb syringe and drops to soften wax. Ask your pharmacist for assistance in your selection. If you can't manage this yourself or you are unsuccessful in removing wax, you may be able to get your ears flushed at your medical clinic. Many clinics offer this service to older adults or can make a referral to an ear, nose, and throat doctor to have the wax removed. Do not try to remove wax from your ears with sharp objects.

Vaccinations

Vaccinations recommended for older adults are listed in the chart below. Some infections can be prevented by vaccines. If your tetanus immunization is up-to-date, you will not get tetanus. Many women are in need of a tetanus booster, because work in the home does not lead to tetanus-prone injury for which men often receive boosters. Men may also have their immunizations more up-to-date because of military service where immunization is mandatory. Vaccination may make diseases like influenza or pneumococcal pneumonia less serious even if you become ill.

Summary

Some of the recommendations for maintaining wellness are easy to give and hard to follow. For example, eat well or exercise regularly sounds quite simple until you try to

Vaccinations Recommended
for People Over 65 Years of Age

Vaccine	Guidelines for Use
Influenza	Yearly in the fall
Pneumococcal	Once at any time
Tetanus	A primary series of three shots in a year, then a booster every 10 years

change your habits. You must work at changing your lifestyle to a more healthy one. Even small improvements can bring large rewards.

References

Some information in this chapter was adopted from the following sources.

Anderson, B. (1980). *Stretching*. Bolinas, CA: Shelter Publications.

Hess, L. V. (1989). Nutritional care of the geriatric patient. *Journal of Home Health Care Practice*, 2(1), 29–38.

Oliverva, O. H. (1987). Living with sleep changes. In *Living with old age* (pp. 95–126). Knoxville, TN: Psychological Services.

Sallade, J. R. (1986). *Exercise for health*. Alexandria, VA: American Physical Therapy Association.

Chapter 4

Activities of Daily Living: Strategies for Independence

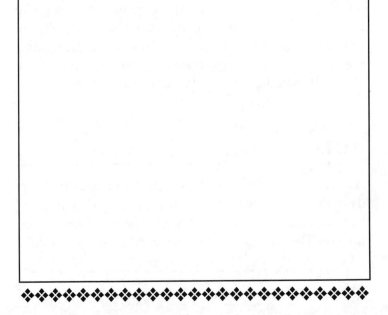

An important goal for the older adult is to maintain functional ability. Functional ability can be determined by an adult's ability to perform activities of daily living (ADLs). ADLs, as explained in Chapter 1, are the common everyday activities of life. As you age, it often becomes more difficult to accomplish daily activities. Depending on the type and severity of your difficulties, you may require the assistance of another person or the use of an adaptive device to accomplish daily tasks.

Any number of conditions may inhibit your ability to perform ADLs. A chronic condition, such as arthritis, can make it progressively more difficult to do things for yourself because of joint pain or loss of joint motion. An acute condition, such as a hip fracture or a degenerative mental disease (like dementia), may also contribute to loss of independence.

This chapter will review strategies you may use to maintain independence in ADLs. There are environmental and physical adaptations available that may improve your abilities to perform daily living tasks. These adaptations generally are simple enough to do on your own. However, some changes require evaluation by professionals who may recommend specific techniques to follow to improve a function.

ADLs

As defined in Chapter 1, ADLs are the basic activities of daily living such as eating, bathing, getting in and out of bed, walking, dressing, and going to the bathroom. Chapter 8 reviews strategies to reduce falls, as well as strategies to assist you with maintaining independence and safety during bathing, using the toilet, walking, and getting in and out of bed. This chapter focuses on eating, dressing, and urinary continence.

Eating

Eating includes the ability to sit for a meal, get the food from the plate to your mouth, and the process of chewing and swallowing your food.

There are several reasons you may have difficulty eating. Listed below are common problems that may cause difficulties and suggestions to help alleviate these problems.

Positioning

Sitting upright is the safest position for eating. Eating in a reclined position can be dangerous, especially if you are experiencing difficulty with swallowing foods or liquids.

If it is difficult for you to sit upright or maintain head control, you may need a referral to an occupational or physical therapist to help with body control. Information on contacting an occupational or physical therapist is found in Chapter 8.

Adaptive Eating Devices

You may experience problems with hand strength, limited arm movement, or decreased coordination that make eating difficult. These problems may make it difficult to grasp eating utensils or bring the food to your mouth. There are a number of devices available that may reduce these difficulties and allow you to eat independently again. Examples of such devices are found in the pictures on pages 48–49.

Large-handled silverware may help people who have a decreased grasp. This difficulty may be caused by arthritic

Adaptive utensils that may help you when eating. Pictured left to right are a large-handled spoon, a side cutter fork, a curved spoon, rocker knives, and a long-handled spoon.

hands that can no longer make a tight fist or weakened hands that tire when grasping silverware for prolonged periods of time. Utensils can be bought ready-made or be built-up using foam tubing.

Weighted silverware may help people who have decreased sensation in their hands or people who experience a tremor (the weight may reduce the tremor and decrease the amount of food spilled). **Curved, swiveled, or long-handled silverware** may help people who, because of loss of joint motion, have difficulty reaching the mouth using

Pictured left to right are a divided plate with plate guard, a T-handled plastic cup, and a scoop plate.

standard eating utensils. **Rocker knives** may help individuals who have had a stroke and, as a result, have use of only one hand.

Lipped plates and **divided plates** make it easier for people who only have use of one hand or who have poor coordination to scoop food onto their spoons. A **plate guard**, which is a semicircular guard attached to the plate, may also help in such cases. **Lightweight plastic cups** are easier to move from the table to your mouth than ceramic cups or glassware. This is especially true for an older adult who has limited hand grip strength or hand or finger deformities caused by arthritis.

A **nonskid mat** or wet washcloth placed under dishes will keep the dish from moving, helping people who have limited use of their hands and who find it difficult keeping their plate in one place.

Adaptive Eating Techniques

Finger foods, such as sandwiches, fruit slices, or cheese and crackers may be helpful for people who find it extremely difficult to manipulate eating utensils. Finger foods may also be easier for an older adult with dementia who becomes too restless to stay seated for an entire meal.

Some older adults find they are no longer able to tolerate three full meals per day, or find that if they try to eat three full meals, it takes them an excessive amount of time to complete the meal. For such people, it may be better to eat several small meals per day rather than three large meals. Pace yourself during meal time. Eat small mouthfuls of food or liquid, chew the food adequately, complete the swallow, and pause before taking another mouthful.

Alert your physician if you experience difficulties with chewing and/or swallowing food or coughing during mealtimes. Such problems with eating present a risk for aspiration. Aspiration is life threatening and occurs when food or liquids pass through the larynx and enter the lungs. Malnutrition and dehydration also may be problems resulting from such difficulties when eating. The physician may make a referral to a speech pathologist or an occupational therapist who will more closely study your swallowing abilities.

Dressing

Getting dressed includes choosing the appropriate clothing for the weather and occasion, putting the clothes on, and fastening the clothing. Physical or degenerative mental illnesses may cause problems in one or all of these areas.

Adaptive Dressing Techniques

If you have poor vision and you find it is difficult to determine what clothes go together, clothing can be tagged by sewing textured material or a button on the lapels or waistbands. By using your sense of touch you can find matched outfits by finding similar textures.

If fastening clothing is difficult, you may want to try adaptive devices such as button hooks or zipper rings (see the picture on p. 53). Another solution to this problem is to replace fasteners with velcro closures. Some national department stores and small companies carry adaptive clothing. There also are patterns available for making your own adaptive clothing.

Jogging suits (or sweat suits) are loose-fitting clothing that are quick and easy to remove. This is often the choice of clothing for people who experience problems with removing their clothes quickly enough to go to the bathroom, who spend much of their day at home in a wheelchair, or who have problems with fastening clothes.

If putting clothes on is a problem, you may benefit from a referral to an occupational therapist. The occupational therapist will evaluate you to identify your problems. Adaptive devices such as dressing sticks, long-handled shoe horns, or sock aids may make getting dressed easier for you (see the picture on p. 54). The occupational therapist can instruct you in how such equipment works or make recommendations on how to improve your abilities.

Urinary Incontinence

Urinary incontinence, the involuntary loss of urine so severe as to cause problems with cleanliness or social activities, is a major problem for older adults. It can be one of the most frustrating aspects in the life of a person who has disability. It is not, however, a natural consequence of aging. Urinary incontinence is a symptom

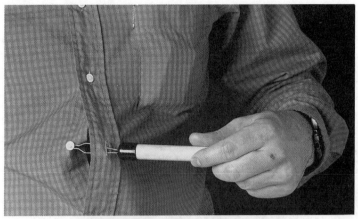

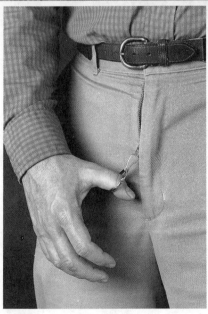

Button hooks and zipper rings are adaptive dressing equipment that can make fastening buttons and zippers easier for you.

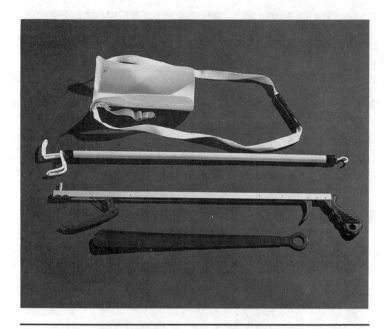

Adaptive dressing equipment that may making dressing easier. Pictured top to bottom are a sock aid, a dressing stick, a reacher, and a long-handled shoe horn.

rather than a disease. If you are experiencing such problems, alert your physician. You can be evaluated to determine the cause and appropriate management.

The sudden onset of incontinence or acute incontinence may be caused by a bladder infection, side effects of medications, restricted mobility—such as from a fracture—a blockage to the normal flow of urine from the bladder caused by a large prostate, constipation, inflammation in the bladder from bladder stones or radiation, or anything else that causes confusion or acute memory problems. Acute incontinence usually resolves when the cause is treated.

When urinary incontinence persists it is called "chronic." The four types of chronic incontinence are stress, urge, overflow, and functional. In older adults, one or more may occur in combination.

Stress Incontinence

Stress incontinence usually involves the involuntary leakage of small to moderate amounts of urine. For this reason stress incontinence often happens with sneezing, coughing, laughing, or picking up heavy objects. Stress incontinence is common in women who have had multiple vaginal births or in males who have had prostatic surgery. Stress incontinence may be treated by drug therapy or behavioral interventions and is sometimes amenable to surgery.

Urge Incontinence

Urge incontinence is the leakage of larger amounts of urine when you can't make it to a toilet after you experience the urge to urinate. This is the type of incontinence usually seen in people who have had strokes, dementia, or other neurological impairments. It can occur if anatomical problems exist, such as a large prostate in men or previous pelvic surgery in women. Urge incontinence may be treated by behavioral interventions, which teach you to control the urge and strengthen the muscles that close the opening of the bladder. There also are medications that can help treat urge incontinence.

Overflow Incontinence

Overflow incontinence is the leakage of urine when there is a mechanical or functional obstruction to the normal flow of urine, and pressure builds up in the bladder to the point that urine is pushed out through the obstruction. You may experience frequent dribbling, which is a common characteristic of overflow incontinence. Often, you have a diminished sensation that your bladder is full and the stream of urine is weak. If overflow is due to a mechanical obstruction such as a large prostate, surgical or medical reduction in the size of the prostate may improve incontinence. If overflow is due to a loss of nerves to the bladder or a weak bladder it may be treated by learning to facilitate bladder emptying, such as pushing on the bladder area while urinating, or learning to insert a soft rubber tube (catheter) into the bladder to empty it. Some medication may be useful in overflow incontinence.

Functional Incontinence

Functional incontinence occurs when you are having difficulty moving from one place to another and cannot hold the urine until you get to the bathroom. Difficulty moving from one place to another may be caused by sensory impairments (decreased vision) or the inability to communicate to your caregiver your need to use the bathroom. Some experts also use the term functional incontinence for incontinence associated with severe dementia. Management of functional incontinence will depend on the cause.

A thorough evaluation of incontinence is important. Talk to your physician about this.

Assistive or Collective Devices for Easier Toileting and Improved Continence

Assistive devices that can improve urinary continence include, but are not limited to, the following:

1. Raised toilet seat (refer to Chapter 8).

2. Toilet frame (refer to Chapter 8).

3. Easy-opening clothing. Examples include sweat suits, velcro-closured clothing (refer to this chapter's section on dressing).

4. Male and female urinals (available through a medical supply company or pharmacy).

5. Bedside commodes (available through a medical supply company or pharmacy).

6. Bedpans (available through a medical supply company or pharmacy).

Techniques to Improve Continence

Caffeine, such as in coffee or tea, can cause urinary frequency or urge incontinence. Alcohol, caffeine, or aspartate contained in products like Nutrasweet® also can contribute to urinary frequency. You may need to cut down your consumption of these items. Your fluid intake should be six to eight 8-ounce glasses per day (unless advised differently by your doctor). If you are awake several times a night to urinate, you may want to drink most of your fluids before 6 p.m.

Preventing constipation will help promote normal bladder function. The easiest way to do this is to eat plenty of fruits, vegetables, whole grains, and beans and to exercise regularly and avoid constipating medications. If you still have problems with constipation or have any change in bowel habits, discuss it with your physician.

Another technique to improve continence in some people is habit training, a technique that establishes a urinating schedule, usually every 2 to 4 hours. The objective of habit training is for you to void before the time of the usual accident rather than to retrain the bladder.

Protective pads, diapers, and undergarments (including condom catheters for males) can provide you with comfort and convenience when experiencing urinary incontinence. You can purchase absorbent pads at most grocery stores, pharmacies, or medical supply centers. This type of intervention should be considered for long-term care only after a thorough evaluation has been done. These supplies are expensive and if they hold moisture against the skin for long periods of time they may lead to pressure sores or infections in the skin.

Urinary incontinence can be distressing and humiliating. It may restrict your daily routine and social outings.

Urinary incontinence is not a normal aging process. If you are experiencing incontinence, alert your physician.

Home Care Programs

When the physical and environmental adaptations described earlier no longer meet your needs and you require assistance with personal cares, a home health agency may be able to help you. Home health agencies provide you with a home health or personal aide who can assist you with your daily living tasks. The use of personal care resources can support independence, maintain people in their own homes, and ease the burden of caring for another.

How to Locate a Home Health Agency

If you feel you would benefit from the assistance of a personal attendant or home health agency, contact one of the following resources:

1. Local hospital or discharge planner.

2. Local or county public health and welfare departments.

3. Social service department.

4. Area Agency on Aging.

5. United Way (lists nonprofit voluntary agencies).

6. Telephone directory (Yellow Pages under "Home Health Services" or "Nurses").

7. Churches/synagogues.

8. Adult day care center.

9. Medical or surgical centers.

10. Nursing homes.

11. Physicians.

Questions to Ask When You Contact a Home Health Agency

Once you have located an agency, there are questions you may want to ask to determine whether the agency would best meet your needs. Listed below are suggested questions to ask.

1. How long has the agency been in business?

2. What is the agency fee?

3. What services are provided?

4. What is the availability of the service (hours/day, days/week)?

5. Is there a minimum time and fee?

6. How does the agency handle payment and billing?

7. Is the agency Medicare/Medicaid certified?

8. Does the fee include supervision by a registered nurse?

9. Is the agency licensed?

10. Is there a waiting list?

The cost of home health care may be covered by Medicare. If you need part-time or intermittent skilled nursing care, physical therapy, or speech therapy, Medicare will provide coverage for these services. If you need intermittent skilled nursing care or physical therapy or speech therapy, Medicare also pays for occupational therapy, medical social services, medical supplies, and for durable medical equipment (80% of the approved amount).

Instrumental Activities of Daily Living (IADLs)

Chapter 1 also referred to the more complex activities of daily living called instrumental activities of daily living (IADLs). These are tasks that you perform on a daily basis that allow you to live in a community setting. An example of an IADL is driving to the grocery store to purchase food to prepare your evening meal. IADLs require a higher level of thinking than the basic survival skills of eating, dressing, or bathing. To complete instrumental tasks, organization, planning, and interaction with your environment is required.

Tasks commonly referred to as IADLs include medication management, financial management, transportation, shopping, meal preparation, laundry, housekeeping, and home maintenance (see the picture on p. 62).

If you have experienced difficulties performing these tasks, you are not alone. Approximately one out of every six older adults experiences difficulties completing instrumental activities without outside help. The most common IADL difficulties include problems getting around the

Grocery shopping is considered an Instrumental Activity of Daily Living that requires planning, organization, and mobility.

community and shopping. To accomplish IADLs, you may find that you need to rely on family or friends or perhaps hire help.

Depending on the size of your community, there may be services or organizations available to help you accomplish IADLs. Often you will find information regarding such services in your local newspaper. Your county human or social service department is another resource to contact for information. See Chapter 10 (Community

Resources for Help at Home section) for information on specific community services that you may find helpful.

Summary

Maintaining functional ability in ADLs and IADLs is the most important goal for the older adult. This ability may allow you to remain in your home. You may be able to maintain independence and avoid unnecessary nursing home stays by using a combination of adaptive equipment and services described in this chapter. Take time now to learn as much as possible about the services available to you for your future peace of mind.

Chapter 5

Regaining Function After Illness or Hospitalization

The greatest impact on functional ability results not from aging itself but from the diseases that occur in people as they age. Eighty percent of people over age 65 have at least one chronic medical illness, and most have more than one. These conditions include heart disease, stroke, arthritis, cancer, diabetes, Alzheimer's disease, and Parkinson's disease. Many acute illnesses are also more likely to occur with advancing age. These include pneumonia, bladder infections, prostate enlargement, and gallbladder stones.

Disease can temporarily or permanently lead to functional impairment through the five "I's" of geriatrics:

1. Immobility

2. Instability (falls and fear of falling)

3. Incontinence (loss of urine or stool involuntarily)

4. Intellectual impairment (usually from stroke or Alzheimer's disease)

5. Iatrogenic illness (illness induced by treatment for another condition; usually from side effects of medications).

These conditions are discussed in more detail in other volumes of the *Coping with Aging* series and other chapters in this volume. This chapter will discuss recovery of health and function after an acute illness.

Recovering Function

After an acute illness or surgery, it is common to become functionally impaired for a variety of reasons. The pain at the site of your surgical incision may make it difficult to sit up. If you lie in bed in a hospital for any length of time, your balance may be shaky and your muscles not as strong as they were before you were sick. You may be on medications, such as those for pain, that make you unsteady on your feet. You may be feeling depressed because you can't do everything you want to do.

Much of this loss of functional ability is temporary, but an older body will take longer to completely recover than a younger body. It is important for you to help your body recover and not to lose further function.

Information You Should Have When You Leave the Hospital or Nursing Home

You should receive written information about your stay in the hospital or nursing home. Information you receive should be in lay language and include:

- Your diagnosis

- Type of operations and complications

- Your doctor's name and how to reach him or her

- Things to watch for and how to be careful in activities

- Instructions for medications, wound care, and diet

- Information on community services that have been arranged for you

- Return appointment times

- Assistance available for transportation

The most popular day for discharge from the hospital is Friday. This may be good if you have family available to help on the weekend. Unfortunately, those health care professionals who know you best may not be available until Monday. If you are unsure of instructions, if the discharge seems sudden, or if there are loose ends in your care needs, resist a discharge on Friday, especially in the afternoon.

Pain

If your illness has involved pain, several areas of concern should be discussed with your physician.

• Will the pain get worse or better?

• Why do you have pain?

• What medications are for your pain?

• What other activities will help to diminish the pain?

• Should you avoid certain activities?

Knowing the answers to these questions will help you work with pain and diminish the amount of pain you have.

Other Unique Problems After Operations

If you had a catheter in your bladder during your hospitalization or nursing home stay, be aware that this can lead to a urinary tract infection even after the catheter is removed. Frequent urination, blood in the urine, or burning with urination are all signs you may be developing a urinary tract infection. If you develop these signs, contact your physician.

Trouble breathing after a hip operation might indicate a blood clot in your lungs. You should talk to your physician about this type of problem. Also note that after an operation your risk for a heart attack will increase for a short while. Therefore, chest pain, fatigue, or heaviness in your chest should not be dismissed. Consult your doctor immediately.

Increase Activity and Exercise

Exercise may be limited when you are recovering from an illness, but anything you can tolerate will be beneficial. You may begin simply by stretching in bed and by moving all joints at least once daily. As you regain more strength, you can begin simple conditioning exercises. Walk as tolerated. If you are just recovering from a fairly long period of bed rest, you should be accompanied by someone and/or have a walking aid (see Chapter 8). If you cannot walk yet, you can do exercises from your bed. For example, you can do simple arm exercises holding soup cans, books, or weights. While you are still in the hospital, ask your doctor to order a consultation with a physical therapist (a specialist typically more involved with lower extremities) or an occupational therapist (a specialist typically more involved with upper extremities) before you are discharged. Ask the therapists to recommend exercises you can do at home. Depending on your need, therapists from home health agencies such as the Visiting Nurse Service can visit you in your home.

Increase Functional Skills

Occasionally, well-intentioned friends and family take over various activities for you because you are in bed and becoming more frail. This can happen also in the hospital or the nursing home where aides and nurses may take over activities of daily living (ADLs) during recovery from an illness. While you are sick or recovering from illness, you may not care to dress or bathe yourself, thinking, "I'm paying for this, I deserve it!" In fact, you need to maintain your function or you will be truly short-changed. Perhaps it will take longer or leave you tired, but your personal effort is important for recovery and for regaining and maintaining function. If the buttons on the shirt don't all get buttoned, be happy for those that do get done; if the bed is half made, that's better than not at all. Sometimes it's better to see the doughnut, not the hole.

Diet is Important to Recover Strength

Good nutrition is critical in regaining function just as in maintaining function; if you are having difficulty eating you may lose body weight. See Chapter 4 for a discussion of aides to use for eating. When you lose too much weight, you also lose muscle. When you lose muscle, you also lose strength.

To prevent weight and muscle loss, eat three meals a day with small snacks in between. Unless you are on a specific therapeutic diet, high-calorie foods with many nutrients like fruit, pudding, crackers with peanut butter, or cereal should be eaten for snacks. Margarine or butter, can be added to foods when additional calories are desired, but may need to be limited if high cholesterol or high fat in the blood is a problem. Dry milk is a good protein source and can be added to cream soup, pudding, or mashed potatoes. It can also be added to pancakes or other similar recipes. Similarly, ice cream, mashed fruit, or flavored syrup can be added to milk. Some people do well with instant breakfast products or canned caloric supplements as a snack item throughout the day. Most older adults should take an inexpensive multiple vitamin tablet daily.

Some Causes of Weight Loss

A list of the causes of weight loss is given in the chart on page 72. Poor dental hygiene is a cause of weight loss that is sometimes overlooked. Consultation with a dentist can help even if a person has no teeth. For a person with painful teeth, some dietary changes can help to improve appetite and weight gain. Soft foods are more easily digested. These include eggs, ground meats, cottage cheese, soft-cooked fruit, pudding, yogurt, or mashed potatoes. You may need to grind, chop, or blend foods. The consistency of baby food is similar to pureed foods and might be appropriate for people who cannot chew food. Hearty soups, stews, and casseroles are appetizing and also easy to digest.

Medications

When recovering from an illness, it is important that you use your medications correctly. To minimize errors in med-

Causes of Weight Loss

Poor teeth

Lack of smell sense

Trouble swallowing

Diarrhea

Depression

Memory problems

Trouble making meals or shopping for food

No money for food

Medications that interfere with appetite

Diseases (examples: diabetes, pulmonary wasting, cancer)

---

ication administration, pills can be set up in advance or monitored by a friend, family member, or other caregiver.

No matter how good a medication is, all medications have potential side effects. When you have been ill and in a hospital or nursing home, the chances are good that you have taken more medications than usual. More medications means more chance for side effects or adverse drug interactions. Experts recommend looking for ways to stop, simplify, or reduce the number of medicines an older adult is taking. The first question you should ask your doctor about any new symptom is, "Could this symptom be caused by my medicine?" Also ask your doctor if there are any medications you are on that you can safely stop or reduce. Do not discontinue medications without your doctor's advice. Nonprescription medications also have side effects. If you are taking over-the-counter medicines or supplemental vitamins tell your doctor.

Summary

When you have been ill, you will have the symptoms of the disease that affects you. You may also become weak because of an illness. You can lose weight, strength, and functional ability that require work to regain. Although it may take older adults longer than younger adults to recover from the insult of an acute illness, the human body has astonishing recuperative abilities. Be patient but persistent in your efforts to regain health and function.

References

Some of the information in this chapter was adapted from the following sources:

Hess, L. V. (1989). Nutritional care of the geriatric patient. *Journal of Home Health Care Practice, 2*(1), 29–38.

Sallade, J. R. (1986). *Exercise for health.* Alexandria, VA: American Physical Therapy Association.

Strauss, A. L. (1975). *Chronic illness and the quality of life.* St. Louis, MO: Mosby.

Suter-Gut, D., Metcalf, A. M., Donnelly, M. A., & Smith, I. M. (1990). Post-discharge care planning and rehabilitation of the elderly surgical patient. *Clinics in Geriatric Medicine, 6*(3), 669–683.

Chapter 6

Coping with Sadness

❖❖❖❖❖❖❖❖❖❖❖❖❖❖❖❖❖❖❖❖❖❖❖❖❖❖❖❖❖❖❖

Sadness and grief are fairly common emotions for older adults. These emotions can result from loss of employment, family, friends, social standing, or health. Sadness and grief are normal human feelings and can be beneficial in some situations. At other times, these emotions can be very strong or prolonged and can become destructive. They can be a part of a mental illness, such as depression, and lead to a decline in functional ability and independence. The causes of sadness, grief, and depression are discussed in this chapter.

Personality Traits Don't Change with Age

A person's personality is not typically affected by aging. A go-getter will still be active and busy. People with a life-long pattern of negative feelings will still be pessimistic. When someone seems sad, unhappy, or depressed it is important to know if these emotions are new.

A change in mood or an apparent change in personality may indicate an illness, such as dementia, that affects the brain. A detailed discussion of dementia is beyond the scope of this book. Dementia will be discussed in detail in another volume in the coping with aging series. Depression (as discussed below), stroke, or other neurological conditions may also cause changes in mood or personality.

In addition, a number of different life situations can lead to sadness. These are discussed in the following sections.

Social Isolation

Social isolation can lead to sadness. Older adults may become less active in community and social groups. This can occur for a variety of reasons, from sickness of a spouse to lack of transportation. In addition, old friends may drift apart because of changes in employment, health, or living arrangements, and opportunities to make new friends may diminish after retirement.

Older adults need to stay involved with other people. Keep going to Rotary Club meetings. Join new groups to broaden your range of interests and meet new people. Take a class. Your experience is needed. There are many support groups for specific illnesses or social circumstances; check these out for your needs. Most communities have senior centers where a variety of activities are available. These activities might include a noon meal followed by bingo, quilting groups, or book clubs. If you can't find an organization to suit your needs and interests, consider starting your own group. Even a person with a memory problem, like Alzheimer's disease, may need to get out, meet people, and stay active. For people with dementia, an adult day center may be an excellent way to prevent social isolation.

Retirement

Most people adjust to retirement fairly well. Work provides something to do, an income, and an identity or purposefulness. The loss of all three of these beneficial aspects of work should be anticipated and planned for prior to retirement. Some people do have difficulty adjusting to retirement. Most of the difficulty adjusting occurs in the first year after retirement and results from lack of planning or unrealistic expectations after retirement. Some people become sick just as they are retiring. As a result, they may feel cheated out of their retirement. See the section below on illness for further information.

Some people find that employment after retirement is fun. They have more to do than ever. Some people take on a new second career. It might be something they always dreamed of doing. People should not retire with the idea of going out to pasture and doing nothing. Activity is important for happiness and also appears to contribute to a longer life.

Parents and Children Change Values and Roles

Aging parents must adjust to their children becoming mature adults. This can be difficult if children have been put in stereotyped roles, like "the baby in the family" or the "black sheep."

When parents become disabled, children may need to assume the role of caregiver. Both children and parents may feel uncomfortable with this role reversal. Losing authority can be equated with loss of respect. This loss can lead to sadness or anger from a parent and resentment from a grown son or daughter who sees a need and is trying to help. Wherever possible you should be encouraged to maintain control of personal and financial matters. The proper balance between safety and autonomy for the older adult requires discussion, respect, and partnership between parents and children.

Illness can Cause Sadness

Illness can lead to sadness for many reasons. You may resent the fact that you are sick—"Why me? Why now?" You may not have the strength or ability to continue usual pastimes. For this reason, it is helpful to maintain multiple interests. For example, loss of vision can diminish your ability to read and the pleasure you derive from reading. Having another hobby not dependent on vision to the same extent, like music, helps.

Illness can lead to a change in personal appearance, for example, hair loss after cancer treatment. You may feel uncomfortable in social gatherings. Illness can lead you to think more about death and dying. However, it's helpful to emphasize what you still *can do*, what you enjoy. A support group may help. Many groups have been organized around particular problems like cancer or diabetes. A close friend, a clergy person, or a health care provider can discuss your fears, frustrations, and sadness. These feelings are a normal reaction to an illness. It's important to express yourself, to clarify your own feelings, and to keep them from festering and becoming harmful.

You may become sad because you are sick, but you can also have difficulty because of the treatment you receive.

See the chart on page 81 for a list of medications that have been reported to cause depression. If you are aware of feeling sad and are taking some of these medicines, talk to your doctor.

Loss of Friends or Spouse

Bereavement is the process of coping with the death of a loved one. It may appear similar to depression. Mourning is a necessary and normal part of bereavement and is associated with grief.

Normal grief behavior is extensive and varied. You may experience anger, sadness, self-reproach, anxiety, or relief. Many people in grief have physical sensations like chest or throat tightness, loss of energy, weakness, dry mouth, or breathlessness. During grief your thinking may be clouded by confusion, disbelief, or preoccupation. Behavior is also affected by the grief reaction. Sleep or appetite may be disturbed. Sighing and crying can occur. In grief you can become absent-minded, restless, or withdrawn.

The extent of mourning depends on the suddenness of the loss, the support you have from others, and the extent to which you can express grief. The process of mourning involves a number of stages. Disbelief, depression, blame, and recovery may occur together and resolve over approximately 6 months to a year. In the latter phases of mourning the feelings mellow. Elderly people are frequently subject to bereavement through the death of multiple lifetime associates, relatives and friends. Each of these losses can be additive and make recovery more difficult.

Some Drugs That Can Cause Depression

Drug (Trade Name)	Medical Use
Acyclovir (Zovirax)	Viral infections
Alcohol	Stimulant
Amphetamine-like drugs: phenylpropanolamine (Dexatrim), diethylpropion (Tenuate), fenfluramine (Pondimin), and others	Colds, weight loss
Asparaginase (Elspar)	Cancer
Baclofen (Lioresal)	Muscle problems
Barbiturates: phenobarbital and others	Sleep, sedation
Benzodiazepines (Valium, Xantax, Tranxene, Ativan, and others)	Anxiety, sleep
Beta-adrenergic blockers: atenolol, propranolol, betaxolol (Kerlone)	Heart disease, high blood pressure, glaucoma
Bromocriptine (Parlodel)	Parkinson's disease
Calcium channel blockers: diltiazem (Cardizem), nifedipine (Procardia)	Heart disease, high blood pressure
Cimetidine (Tagamet)	Stomach problems

(continued)

Some Drugs That Can Cause Depression *(cont'd)*

Drug (Trade Name)	*Medical Use*
Clonidine (Catapres)	High blood pressure
Dapsone	Skin disease
Digoxin (Lanoxin)	Heart disease
Disopyramide (Norpace)	Heart disease
Disulfiram (Antabuse)	Alcoholism
Etretinate (Tegison)	Skin conditions
Halothane (Fluothane)	Anesthetic
Interferon alpha (Roferon-A, Intron A)	Infections
Isotretinoin (Accutane)	Skin conditions
Levodopa (Dopar)	Parkinson's disease
Methyldopa (Aldomet)	Hypertension
Metoclopramide (Reglan)	Stomach disorders
Metrizamide (Amipaque)	For X-rays
Metronidazole (Flagyl)	Infections
Nalidixic acid (Neg Gram)	Infections
Narcotics: codeine, morphine, propoxyphene (Darvon)	Pain

(continued)

Some Drugs That Can Cause Depression *(cont'd)*

Drug *(Trade Name)*	Medical Use
Nonsteroidal anti-inflammatory agents: ibuprofen (Motrin), indomethacin (Indocin), naproxen (Anaprox, Naprosyn), flurbiprofen (Ansaid)	Arthritis, pain
Norfloxacin (Noroxin)	Infections
Pergolide (Permax)	Parkinson's disease
Phenylephrine (Neo-Synephrine)	Nasal congestion
Prazosin (Minipress)	High blood pressure
Reserpine (Serpasil)	Hypertension
Steroids: anabolic, oral contraceptives, prednisone, cortisone, ACTH	Many conditions
Trichlormethiazide (Naqua)	Fluid retention
Trimethoprim-sulfamethoxazole (Bactrim, Septra)	Infection
Tuberculous agents: cycloserine (Seromycin), ethionamide (Trecator-SC), isoniazid (INH)	Tuberculosis treatment

Tasks You Must Accomplish to Recover From Mourning

There are four tasks that you complete when mourning. The first task is acceptance of the reality of the loss. You must overcome denial and disbelief that death has occurred. The second task is to experience or work through the pain of the grief. Not everyone experiences the pain of grief in the same way, but if you lose someone you are attached to there will be some level of pain. The third task is to adjust to the deceased person being gone. You must come to terms with living alone, an empty house, no one to call, or whatever. You must adapt to the loss. Finally, you must take the emotional energy from your relationship to the deceased person and reinvest it in another relationship. Reinvestment is difficult. It takes time, but you need to love and be loved. This does not mean you love the deceased person any less.

It may not be easy to accomplish these tasks while you are grieving. As in depression discussed below, you may need professional help to work through the loss of friends or spouse.

Depression

All people are subject to swings in mood, to highs and lows, ups and downs in feelings. In depression, the person has a prolonged period (more than 2 weeks) of symptoms. The symptoms of depression are of a psychological and physical nature as listed in the chart on page 85.

Symptoms of Depression

Psychological

Inability to enjoy anything
Persistent sad, anxious, or empty mood
Thoughts of death or suicide
Feelings of hopelessness, worthlessness, or pessimism

Physical

Problems sleeping—either insomnia or oversleeping
Loss of or increased appetite
Weight loss or gain
Constipation
Fatigue, irritability, or trouble concentrating

Physical symptoms include change in the sleep pattern, a change in bowel habits (usually constipation), loss of interest in sexual activity, low energy level, or appetite change. Psychological symptoms can be quite diverse. Depressed people may not enjoy doing things they previously liked. They may not be able to take pleasure from anything. They may unexpectedly change their wills, be preoccupied with morbid thoughts, or consider suicide. Crying spells may be frequent. These crying spells are associated with sadness.

Sometimes depression can cause memory problems and difficulty concentrating. This can mimic the memory problems of dementia. Some people with depression may have a variety of physical complaints that have no other demonstrable cause. These include chest or abdominal problems, pain in any body part, or crawling sensations under the skin. Other psychological symptoms that may be found in people with depression include feelings of excessive guilt about past life events, a sense of worthlessness or low self-esteem, anxiety, and a sense of helplessness about life situations.

These symptoms are not part of the normal aging process and should not be attributed to "getting older." A wide variety of medical conditions can cause depression. These include problems with function of some of the endocrine glands, infections, cancer, and internal organ failure such as heart failure or kidney disease. Alcohol and many prescription medications listed in the chart on page 81 can also cause depression. Treating the underlying illness or taking away the offending medication may well lead to recovery.

The pervasive sadness of the depressed person affects those around them. When you leave a person and come away feeling sad or depressed yourself, it's a good clue that the person you were with is depressed, and a medical opinion should be sought.

Treatment for Depression

Depressed people need professional help. The primary care physician often can help the depressed person. In some situations, psychiatric or social work consultation is important for diagnosis or treatment. If your primary care physician can't refer you to these professionals, check with your local medical society (see Chapter 2). It may be hard for some people to seek help because of the stigma associated with being perceived as "crazy." A mental health problem does not indicate a character flaw. It simply means you are ill. Several different antidepressant medicines are effective for depression. People with mild depression may respond well to psychotherapy or counseling. This is especially true for older adults with a strong sense of helplessness or other psychological symptoms of depression. Helping older adults to cope with loss can be pivotal in the psychotherapy process. When the symptoms of depression are life threatening, older adults can respond rapidly to electroconvulsive "shock" therapy. Electroconvulsive therapy sounds frightening, but it is not the horror depicted in movies and the lay press. This therapy can be life saving in the severely depressed patient in whom it may not be safe to wait the several weeks needed for response to medication.

Summary

Sadness, grief, and depression can all occur as you get older. When the emotions are not overpowering and you recognize the cause, it may be possible to handle the situation yourself. If you have questions about your symptoms, or difficulty because of them, help is available for you. Don't be afraid to seek it.

References

Some information in this chapter was adapted from the following sources.

Edinberg, M. A. (1985). *Mental health practice with the elderly.* Englewood Cliffs, NJ: Prentice-Hall.

Frank, J. (1983). Illness and invulnerability. *New England Journal of Medicine, 308,* 1268–1274.

Hurlock, E. B. (1980). *Developmental psychology: A life span approach* (5th ed.). New York: McGraw-Hill.

Stevens-Long, J. (1984). *Adult life* (2nd ed.). Palo Alto, CA: Mayfield.

Chapter 7

Coping with Arthritis

Arthritis is the most common cause of chronic illness in older adults. It affects a third of those over 45 years of age and half or more of those over 60 years of age. Degenerative arthritis is the most common type of arthritis that affects older adults. In this chapter the focus is on degenerative arthritis and how to cope with it.

What is Degenerative Arthritis?

Degenerative arthritis is known by several names including osteoarthritis or degenerative joint disease. Degenerative arthritis is caused by the breakdown of cartilage in the joint. The primary symptom of degenerative arthritis is pain. The pain in degenerative arthritis occurs in joints, most commonly the knees, hips, spine, and hands. Joints that have been injured in the past are particularly susceptible to degenerative arthritis. Often, people develop deformity of the joints from degenerative arthritis. When a joint is painful or deformed, it becomes functionally impaired. For example, simple household chores, taking a walk, or getting a good night's rest may be difficult. You can get more information about degenerative arthritis or the other types of arthritis from the Arthritis Foundation. Write to them at 3400 Peachtree Road, N.E., Atlanta, GA 30326 to find out if there is a local arthritis chapter near you.

What Causes Pain in Arthritis?

Arthritis pain can be caused by inflammation. When inflammation occurs, structures surrounding the joint also can become inflamed and painful. The surrounding structures of the joint include tendons, ligaments, and bursa. Bursa are fluid-filled sacks or spaces around joints that help joint parts slide over one another. When a bursa is inflamed, it is referred to as bursitis.

Pain also can be caused by mechanical stress around the joint. Mechanical stress occurs in arthritis because the joint becomes deformed as the arthritis progresses. Deformity is most obvious when the joint can no longer be fully straightened or bent. Pain caused by mechanical stress occurs when the joint is used. For example, degenerative arthritis of the hip or knee is painful during walking. When degenerative arthritis affects the spine, nerves can be affected. If a nerve in your neck is pinched, pain, tingling, or numbness in the hand or arm may occur. If a nerve in the lower back is affected, then these symptoms may develop in the leg or foot.

What Can You do About Degenerative Arthritis?

There are a number of things you can do to take care of your arthritis (see the chart on page 92). The most important is to maintain flexibility, strength, posture, and gait and to avoid injury to joints. People who sit a great deal lose flexibility of the knees and hips. This can lead to pain when walking or an abnormal gait. Sitting in a round-shoulder position is stressful for your back and neck, so good posture is a must. Poor posture leads to unnecessary muscle tension and greater energy use. At a minimum, older adults should stand, walk, lift their arms,

Treatment of Degenerative Arthritis

Goal	*Treatment*
Maintain or improve flexibility and strength	Stretching and exercise, energy conservation (good posture and work conditions)
Eliminate inflammation	Limit activity, anti-inflammatory medicine, physical modalities
Remove mechanical stress or deformity	Joint protection, pain medication, surgical treatment

rotate hips, turn, and straighten their legs three times a day. Many people should engage in an active exercise program because of the broad benefits that result (see the chart on p. 93). See Chapter 3 for a basic exercise program. You may need to adapt your exercise program to your degree of disability and to the particular joints most affected. Respect pain and fatigue; if they occur, you may injure yourself.

When arthritis is complicated by inflammation, the joint will hurt most of the time even if you are inactive. If this is a problem, consult a physician. The physician will make sure the inflammation is not caused by an infection in the joint. If the inflammation is caused by arthritis, you may need to limit activity for a week or so until the pain decreases. A physical therapist can be helpful in recom-

Benefits of an Exercise Program

Improved flexibility

Increased endurance to activity

Prevent loss of strength

Improved sense of well-being

Decrease muscular or skeletal pain

Improved balance and coordination

mending treatment. A splint or brace may be helpful to limit use or protect an inflamed joint. A physical therapist may recommend or use such treatments as heat, cold, ultrasound, immersion into warm wax, or range-of-motion exercises. Medical treatments for inflamed joints include anti-inflammatory medicines, injection of corticosteroids into affected joints, or surgery. Surgery is considered a last resort for severe impairment or pain, but can offer dramatic improvements in certain cases.

Joint Protection

The joint becomes deformed from the destructive process of the arthritis. On top of this are added the external forces resulting from the stresses put on the joint during normal daily activity. Joint protection is the technique used to reduce external stress on damaged joints. For example, with arthritis in the knees, walking in a swimming pool takes some of the strain off the knees. For people with arthritis in their neck, it is important to sleep with the head in a neutral position (see the illustration on p. 95). This keeps strain off the neck joints. Good posture during sleep can be maintained with a cervical pillow. You may need to adjust the position of your arms or legs when falling asleep or during the night to maintain good neck position throughout the night. Also avoid forcing your neck into a position that hurts. Even holding your neck in an awkward position while dusting upper cupboards, cleaning, or painting can cause an arthritis flare up.

Strengthen the Joint

Keeping the muscle around the joint strong helps take some of the strain off the joints themselves. This is why exercise is so helpful. When the joint becomes deformed, muscle strength may not be as helpful unless a splint is used to help realign the bones and the joint. In some cases a splint, brace, cane, walker, crutches, wheelchair, or other device may be needed to protect and rest the arthritic joint. See Chapter 8 for more joint protection ideas you can use in your home.

Posture and Position are Important for Energy Conservation

Good posture and work position are important to avoid fatigue. When standing or sitting, your shoulders should be back (not shrugged) and your head held upright— "Throw your chest out." When you work standing at a

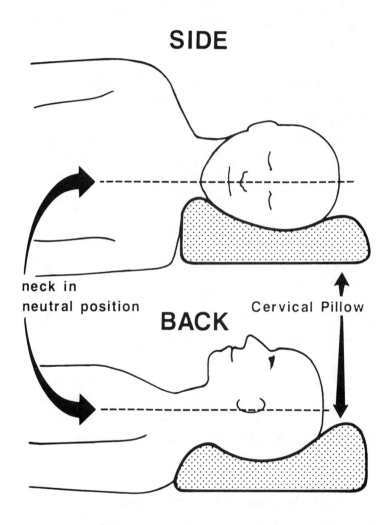

Use a cervical pillow to keep your neck in a neutral position when lying on your side or back.

table, make certain you stand tall. Don't bend forward over your work. The correct working height when standing at a table is with your elbows 2 inches above the tabletop. The table should be at least waist high. If necessary, put blocks under the legs of the table to get the correct height. Excessive bending forward can occur when you wash a sink full of dishes. To eliminate excessive bending, wash some dishes now and some later. It also can be helpful to keep a footstool by the sink or open the cupboard door under the sink and rest one foot or the other on a higher level, thereby changing your position while you work. Some people will benefit from a pad underfoot to soften the hard floor.

Don't hold the same position for prolonged periods of time. This causes muscle fatigue. When the muscle is tired, more stress is placed on the weakened joint. This may occur while reading, watching TV, working at the counter or sink, or writing for longer than 10 minutes. Change your position often to relax your muscles. Sit instead of standing for any job requiring 10 minutes or longer.

All of these ideas are designed to conserve energy and avoid fatigue. You may recognize other body positions you assume during the week that are energy draining. Can you modify your position or activity to save energy? If so, you will get more work done and feel better.

Use Body Mechanics to Advantage

Applying principles of body mechanics can help protect your joints (see the chart on p. 97). Use the strongest or

Joint Protection Behavior

Lift using knees, not back

Carry using forearms, not hands

Carry using both hands, palms up, not one hand

Push heavy things

Slide objects or add wheels to them

Avoid tight grasp

Avoid prolonged periods in the same position

largest joints available for the job. Use your knees, not your back, for heavy lifting. When carrying a handbag, don't put the strap in your clenched hand, put the strap over your forearm or shoulder. This takes the pressure off your hand and wrist and places it instead on the larger, stronger elbow or shoulder.

It also is helpful to slide objects rather than lift and to push heavy things rather than to lift or pull them. When you push the chair or sofa you use your hips and shoulders rather than your hands and back. Some household objects can be put on wheels to make sliding easier. Vacuuming rugs is hard on the back because it involves a bent forward posture and pulling motion. People with back problems should limit the amount of vacuuming they do.

For the hand or wrist with arthritis, a number of motions or positions should be avoided. The illustrations on page 98 show several examples of wrong and right ways to use

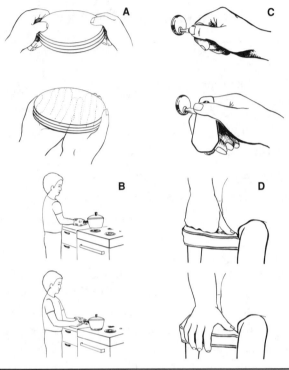

Joint protection ideas to lessen the stress on fingers and
wrist. The incorrect position is demonstrated in the
upper panel, and the correct position is demonstrated
in the lower panel. A) Use your whole hands and arms
when lifting, not just your fingers and wrists. B) Slide
pots across the stove, and use both arms. C) Use a
lever arm on your key to lessen the strain of turning
the key in the lock. D) Support your weight with an
open hand, not a closed fist. (Adapted from Furst, G.,
Gerber, L. H., Smith, C., 1985, *Rehabilitation through
learning: Energy conservation and joint protection.*
Bethesda, MD: U.S. Department of Health and
Human Services, National Institute of Health.)

your hands and wrists. The correct technique is shown in the lower panels. Do not support objects with your fingers alone when lifting (illustration A). Scoop up objects such as kitchen plates or packages with both hands, keeping palms underneath to support the object you are lifting. When moving pots or kettles off the stove use both hands and use sliding motions rather than lifting (illustration B). Tight grasping, such as when using a screwdriver, carrying a heavy pail, or trying to unscrew a tight jar lid can be hard on hands and wrists. To avoid the tight grasp, release your grasp frequently while working. Build up the grip on a pencil or screwdriver with foam, tape, or commercially available devices to make the turning motion easier. Use a lever arm for turning a key or the door handle to relieve pressure on your hand (illustration C). Ask for consultation with an occupational therapist to obtain the best mechanical aide for you (see Chapter 4). When supporting yourself in a standing position, or to change positions from seated to standing or vice versa, use your open hand for support (illustration D). This distributes the work away from your wrist and fingers to the forearm and shoulder.

An excellent guide to joint protection is available from the Clinical Center Office of Clinical Reports and Inquiries, NIH, Bethesda, MD 20205, (301) 496-2563, entitled *Rehabilitation Through Learning: Energy Conservation and Joint Protection.*

Summary

Degenerative arthritis is common in older adults. It can cause pain, fatigue, and loss of function. This chapter discussed medical treatment, physical therapy, energy conservation, and body mechanics. All of these will help you cope with arthritis.

References

Some information in this chapter was adapted from the following sources.

Arthritis Foundation. *Osteoarthritis. A handbook for patients.* Atlanta, GA: Author.

Bernstein, L. C., & Bottomley, J. M. (1990). Musculoskeletal changes with age. In L. C. Bernstein (Ed.), *Aging: The health care challenge* (2nd ed, pp. 135–161). Philadelphia, PA: F.A. Davis.

Furst, G., Gerber, L. H., & Smith, C. (1985). *Rehabilitation through learning: Energy conservation and joint protection.* Bethesda, MD: U.S. Department of Health and Human Services, National Institutes of Health.

Chapter 8

Falls and Safety

Falls are the most common accident with older adults, and falls occur most often at home. Falls can cause injuries that could lead to disability. They can result in fractured hips, the need to use walking aids such as canes or walkers, or fear of falling again.

What causes falls? What can be done to prevent falls from occurring? This chapter will discuss some of the reasons people fall, what you can do to reduce the risks of falling in your home, what types of devices can help prevent falls, and which professionals to contact if falling is a problem.

Why Do People Fall?

Falls can be caused by a variety of factors, which can be broken down into two general categories: intrinsic and extrinsic. Intrinsic factors are usually health problems in the person who falls. Extrinsic factors are usually obstacles in the environment.

Intrinsic Factors: Medical and Physical

Intrinsic factors include weakness from any illness, loss of vision or hearing, a fall in blood pressure when changing positions, changes in posture, joint deformities, or disturbances in gait or balance.

Acute illnesses such as an infection, dehydration, or a metabolic imbalance are intrinsic factors that may temporarily have an affect on balance and gait.

Chronic diseases that can cause gait changes and increase the likelihood of falls include Parkinson's disease, arthritis, stroke, dementia, cardiac disease, and foot problems. A painful bunion, for example, can make you unsteady when you walk.

A drop in blood pressure because of a change in position, such as when changing from a lying to sitting or sitting to standing position, is called orthostatic hypotension. This occurs in up to 25 percent of older adults. This blood pressure drop can cause dizziness, which may cause you to lose your balance and possibly fall.

Alcohol use may also contribute to falls. Problems with gait or balance may worsen with the use of alcohol, increasing the risk of falls. For anyone who is already at risk of falling, abstaining from alcohol is the best recommendation to reduce the risk.

Many older adults use prescription medications, which may affect such intrinsic factors as balance or cause orthostatic hypotension. Your physician should evaluate your medication use and any possible side effects to determine if they could put you at risk of falling.

How to Cope with Intrinsic Risk Factors for Falls

Intrinsic factors often are not reversible, and one must learn techniques to compensate and cope with a given problem. For example, joint pain and a decrease in energy level commonly accompany arthritis. However, many people who have arthritis continue to lead active life-styles. They do this by learning techniques to compensate for their loss of energy, such as changing daily routines to conserve energy or using walking devices to protect joints, and incorporating these changes into their daily lives (see Chapter 7). Other compensatory techniques include exercise programs, medication changes, and obtaining services from outside agencies to help with daily activities.

An individual may have a variety of intrinsic factors that contribute to the risk of falling. The more intrinsic factors, the greater your risk of falls. Your physician must evaluate each of these factors to determine appropriate interventions and compensatory techniques.

Extrinsic Factors

Extrinsic factors that can contribute to falls are primarily environmental obstacles such as uneven floor surfaces, poor lighting, cluttered pathways, throw rugs, exposed electrical wires, or telephone cords. It often is easier to change an extrinsic factor, in order to reduce falls, than it is to change an intrinsic factor.

The next section of this chapter will focus on the environmental obstacles found within homes, since the home is where falls occur most frequently, and because there are steps you can take to make your home safer.

Safety Within Your Home

Take a close look at your home to see if you can make changes that will increase your safety. Check your home for the following 10 conditions in the Home Safety Checklist.

Home Safety Checklist

This checklist was adapted from the Home Safety Checklist developed by Jane H. Williams, OTR, of the Hospital Based Home Care Program at the William S. Middleton Memorial Veteran's Hospital, Madison, WI.

1. Are all carpets and throw rugs slip-resistant, with edges secured to prevent tripping?

2. Are light switches easy to reach when entering a room?

3. Do stairs have securely fastened handrails?

4. Do you have smoke alarms installed?

5. Do you have emergency numbers listed next to the phone?

6. Are hallways and stairways well lit?

7. Are outside steps well lit, free of snow, and uncluttered?

8. Is your hot water heater set at 120 degrees or lower to prevent burns?

9. Are items you need within easy reach so there is no need for use of a stool or ladder?

10. Are the furnace and the house wiring in good repair?

Any questions to which you answered "no" are safety hazards in your home. Correcting these situations will reduce your risk for accidents such as falls.

Home Safety to Reduce the Risk of Falls

With some foresight, you can change your home to make it safer and reduce your risk of falling. Some of these changes are simple and inexpensive. Others require the knowledge and skill of an architect or a contractor.

Here are some suggestions to make your home safer. The suggested changes are organized by living areas in your home, although some suggestions can be generalized to other living areas.

Stairs

1. Stairwells should be well lit. There should be a light switch located at the top and bottom of the stairwell to prevent having to negotiate in a darkened hallway.

2. Stairwells should have securely fastened handrails on both sides of the stairs to help you negotiate the stairs safely. Install the handrails approximately 30 inches from the stair and set out from the wall far enough to allow for a good grasp.

3. If you are experiencing visual changes, it may be difficult to discriminate the edge of a stair, especially the first and last step. You can mark these steps with a contrasting color, such as a brightly colored tape. Yellow is probably the best color to use because it is a color seen well by the aging eye.

Hallways and Other Rooms

1. Clear all pathways of clutter. Remove all electrical wires or telephone cords that cross the pathway.

2. Throw rugs are often the cause of a fall. The best solution is to remove all throw rugs. If you don't remove them, make sure they are fastened securely by having a nonskid surface below the rug or by taping the edges.

3. Flooring surfaces are another factor in the safety of your home. A highly polished floor surface, whether it is vinyl or ceramic tile, can be hazardous. Glare can be mistaken for water or an uneven floor surface and cause falls. Solutions to eliminate these hazards include not waxing the vinyl flooring or using a wax with minimal buffing to prevent slipping. Unglazed ceramic tiles are slip-resistant when wet and reduce your risk of falls.

Thick pile carpets may lead to tripping and slipping, or they may catch the tip(s) of your walking device. The best type of carpet to install in your home is one of low pile. This will make it easier and safer to walk or negotiate with a wheelchair.

Bathroom

There are many changes you can make to increase your safety in the bathroom. The equipment shown in the pictures, as well as other suggested changes, are described for you below.

1. A rubber mat with suction cups or adhesive strips should be placed on the bottom surface of the bathtub to prevent you from slipping.

2. A grab bar is a hand rail that is used to provide support and stability (see the picture on p. 108). People often use the towel rack or soap dish for stability. These

A grab bar provides stability and increases safety for a person during the activity of bathing. A grab rail fits over the edge of the bathtub to provide a secure hand hold when getting into and out of the tub. Hand-held showers increase the ease and efficiency of showering. This is a hand-held shower with a wall-mount.

are not designed to hold the weight of a person and may give way! Installing grab bars in the bathtub and near the toilet will provide you with such support and stability.

Grab bars need to be installed into the studs of the wall to provide adequate support. If you rent the home or apartment in which you live, you will need to contact the manager for approval before you install the grab bars. You may need to contact a professional to install the grab bars if you are unable to locate the wall studs or lack the proper tools or skills.

Grab bars are available in varying lengths. Most grab bars are straight, although there are angled grab bars. The best shape for your bathroom depends on the available space. Some grab bars are available with a textured surface that may be easier to hold onto when your hands are wet.

Grab bars can be purchased at home improvement centers, hardware stores (in the plumbing section), at local pharmacies that carry durable medical equipment, or through adaptive equipment catalogs.

You may not be able to install a grab bar if the property manager does not allow it, if you are unable to locate the studs of the wall, if you live in a trailer home, or have a modular bathtub.

3. A grab rail is a hand support that is mounted on the tub rail (see the picture on p. 108). If a grab bar is not possible, a grab rail is another alternative to provide stability. Grab rails can be purchased at local pharmacies that carry durable medical equipment or through adaptive equipment catalogs. One advantage to a grab rail is that it is easy to remove and install if you need to relocate. Grab rails cannot be used with bathtubs that have sliding glass doors.

4. Hand-held showers make it easier to control the spray of water and to wash more efficiently, because you will expend less energy (see the picture on p. 108). A hand-held shower can be used to convert a tub into a shower when using a bath seat or bench. Diverter valves are available to change an existing shower head into a hand-held shower.

Hand-held showers can be purchased at home improvement centers, hardware stores (in the plumbing section), at local pharmacies that carry durable medical equipment, or through adaptive equipment catalogs. You may need to hire a plumber to install certain types of handheld showers, depending on your existing system.

5. A bath seat or bath bench is a plastic seat (with rubber-tipped legs) that fits inside the bathtub. A bath seat or bath bench allows you to sit safely while showering and may help you prevent falls. By sitting on the seat or bench you eliminate the need for excessive bending and reaching, and you save energy.

The difference between a bath seat (see the picture on p. 111) and a bath bench (see the picture on p. 111) is that the bath seat fits entirely inside the bathtub, but the bath bench has a section that sets over the edge of the tub. A bath bench is especially beneficial if you are experiencing difficulties lifting your legs over the edge of the tub when getting in or out.

Bath seats and benches can be purchased at local pharmacies that carry durable medical equipment, or through adaptive equipment catalogs. A bath bench is generally more expensive than a bath seat.

6. A raised (or elevated) toilet seat is an attachment that adds height to your existing toilet. Raised (or elevated) toilet seats can increase the height of the seating surface 2 to 4 inches (see the picture on p. 112), making it easier to get on and off the toilet. Toilet seats are easily removable for other family members or guests.

Raised toilet seats can be purchased at local pharmacies that carry durable medical equipment, or through adaptive equipment catalogs.

A bath seat fits inside of the bath or shower to allow a
person to sit for increased safety.

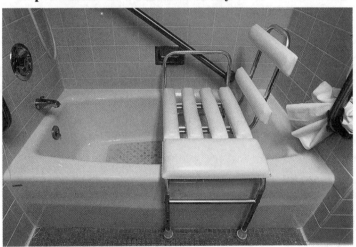

A bath bench provides a method for level, safe transfers
for people who have difficulty with raising their legs
into and out of the tub.

Sitting and standing is easier with an elevated toilet seat.

7. A toilet seat frame, or safety frame, is a set of armrests that attach to the structure of the toilet or are attached directly to the raised toilet seat. Toilet seat frames, or safety frames, provide support and stability when getting on or off the toilet (see the picture on p. 113). They act as the arms of a chair.

These safety frames can be purchased at local pharmacies that carry durable medical equipment, or through adaptive equipment catalogs.

8. A long-handled sponge is a round sponge on the end of a 24-inch flexible handle. Long-handled sponges can eliminate the need for excessive bending and reaching when bathing. They allow you to clean those difficult to reach places, such as your back, legs, or feet.

A toilet safety frame provides steady support for transfers on and off the toilet.

Long-handled sponges can be purchased at retail stores or through adaptive equipment catalogs.

Seating Surfaces: Beds, Chairs, or Sofas

Getting on and off a bed or in and out of a chair may be difficult for some older adults. Everyone has experienced difficulty getting up from a low, soft sofa. Here are some simple changes that can make this movement easier for you and lower your risk of falling.

1. The height of a bed or chair can make a big difference in the ease or difficulty of getting up.

The optimal seat height is the popliteal height, which is the distance from the floor (with your foot firmly planted on the floor) to the space behind your knee (when your knee and hips are bent at right angles) as shown in the picture below. A general rule of thumb is that the height of a chair or bed should be approximately 17–18 inches, and the mattress or chair cushion should have firm edges that don't sag when you stand up. It is easiest to stand up from a seat that is at popliteal height, or higher.

2. To have seating surfaces equal to or higher than popliteal height, place wooden block risers underneath

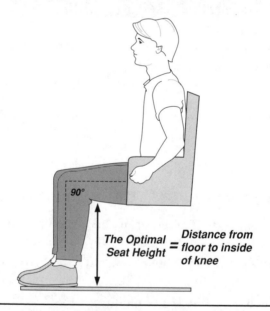

90°

The Optimal Seat Height = Distance from floor to inside of knee

---

The optimal seat height, or the popliteal height, is the measured distance from the floor to the space behind the knee.

---

the legs of the bed, chair, or sofa. You could increase the height of a bed surface by placing an air or egg-crate mattress on top of the existing mattress. To increase the seating surface height on a chair or sofa, add a firm foam cushion on top of the cushion that is already there.

3. Make sure the surface of the bed, chair, or sofa is firm rather than soft. Firm surfaces make it easier to support your weight and balance yourself when you get up. You can make the surface firmer by placing a piece of plywood underneath the mattress or cushion.

4. Getting out of a bed or chair may be difficult for you. Trapezes above the head of the bed (see the picture on p. 116), bed hoists, or grab rails may make getting in and out of bed easier. A chair with arms will be much easier and safer to get in or out of than a chair without arms because the arms provide you with leverage during sitting or rising.

5. The position of your body when getting out of bed or a chair can make a difference in how easy or hard it is. Always remember to bring your buttocks as close to the edge of the seating surface as possible. Plant your feet firmly on the floor, shoulder width apart. Lean your head and trunk forward over your knees. Push yourself forward and upright with your arms and legs to stand from the seating surface. All of these moves will make standing/rising easier (see the picture on p. 116).

General Suggestions for Home Safety

1. It's a good idea to prepare a plan of escape from your home in the case of a fire. This is even more important

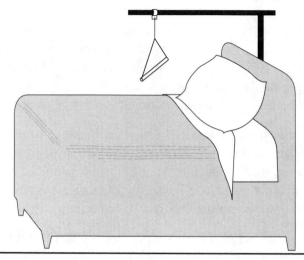

A trapeze above the bed provides leverage for more effective movement when in bed.

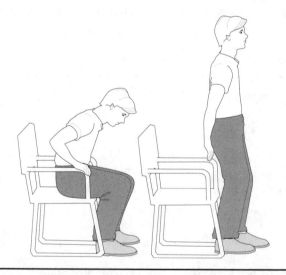

Optimal body position when moving from sit to stand is feet shoulder-width apart, head over knees, with forward momentum.

for the older adult who is bedridden or severely limited in mobility.

2. To prevent burns, the water heater is best set at 120 degrees Fahrenheit or lower. A fall in the bathtub or shower with hot water running can result in a burn to the skin. Ninety percent of severe burns in the home occur in the bathtub or shower. Many hot water heaters are set at 150 degrees Fahrenheit, which will cause a blistering scald in 5 seconds—faster than you can pull your hand from under the water.

3. To improve nighttime vision and reduce confusion if you have to get up, place a night light in the bathroom or other areas of the house.

4. Place frequently used items on a cupboard that is at a level between your shoulders and hips to avoid excessive bending and reaching.

In addition to making your home safer, these changes may also make it easier for you to remain in your home, if you become physically or mentally impaired.

Professionals Who Can Help

The changes just suggested are a few examples of how to increase your safety within your home and prevent falls. If you continue to have falls or experience problems with moving about safely within your home, you may need to contact professionals to help you evaluate and solve the problem. The following professionals can help you.

Your Physician

Your physician may evaluate your physical health and well-being, review your medications, or refer you to other health care professionals (e.g., physical or occupational therapists) for further evaluation and treatment.

A Physical Therapist

A physical therapist (PT) will assess how you walk or move and test your balance, strength, and motor coordination to determine if there is a device to increase your mobility and safety. A PT will also instruct you in proper use of the device and may set up guidelines for a walking or exercise program. You can contact a physical therapist by asking your doctor for a recommendation or looking in the yellow pages of your telephone book under the headings of physical therapy, rehabilitation, or therapy departments of local hospitals. Physical therapists can practice without a physician's referral in some states. However, a referral from your doctor may be necessary to have the services of a physical therapist covered by your insurance.

An Occupational Therapist

An occupational therapist (OT) will assess your mobility, balance, strength, and motor coordination while you perform your daily activities. OTs take into account your sensory systems—that is your hearing, vision, and touch—to determine what types of assistive devices could increase your safety and independence. They may also assess your home environment for barriers. You need a physician's referral to see an occupational therapist.

All of these health care professionals can make suggestions that are specific to you and your home to increase safety and mobility.

Walking Devices

A number of devices are available to assist you with walking safely inside and outside of your home. There are different varieties of each device. Your physician or therapist will help determine what works best for you. The cost of such devices varies; the more complex the device the higher the cost. Medicare or private insurance *may* pay for such devices, although often such coverage is limited or not provided. Your physician or therapist should be able to tell you what financial assistance is available for purchasing these assistive devices.

The three basic types of walking devices are canes, walkers, and crutches. These devices can assist you in walking, increase your safety, and help alleviate falls when used appropriately. Each device has its advantages and disadvantages, depending upon your physical abilities.

It is important to have an evaluation by a therapist to determine the appropriate walking device for you and to learn how to use it safely and appropriately.

Canes

Canes are generally used by people who have minor problems with balance, who have mild muscle weakness, or who need to decrease the weight on a leg up to 30 percent. A cane is used in the hand opposite the involved leg. For example, if you were having problems with your right knee, you would use the cane in your left hand. A cane is at the appropriate height when the top of the cane hits the wrist area when the your arm is hung loosely at your side. There should be a rubber tip on the end of the cane to prevent slipping.

Walkers

Walkers are used by people who need more support and stability than a cane can provide or who are required to decrease the weight they are placing on weight-bearing joints like hips or knees.

There are two types of walkers—a standard walker that needs to be picked up off of the floor and moved ahead and a rolling walker (see the picture on p. 121). Rolling walkers often are used by people who experience breathing problems when walking, people who have limitation or pain in their shoulders that makes picking up a standard walker difficult, or people who are unsteady on their feet and are fearful of falling.

Crutches

Crutches are used by people who need to decrease the weight on one or both legs to some extent. There are several techniques for walking with crutches. Your diagnosis will determine what technique is appropriate. The person who issues you crutches (whether it is the physician in

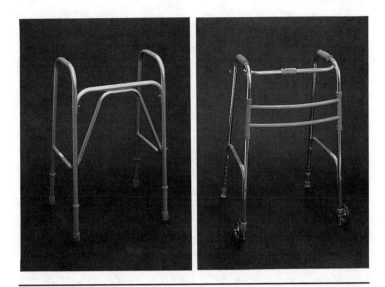

A standard, or four legged, walker and a rolling walker are common devices used to assist a person when walking.

the emergency room or a physical therapist) should instruct you in the proper techniques of crutch walking.

Shoes

Although shoes are not technically walking devices, it is important to always wear sturdy, supportive shoes when walking. Shoes with rubber soles are less likely to slip on flooring surfaces. Be sure that the shoes fit properly and are not causing any sores or areas of pressure.

Foot problems such as bunions or hammertoes require shoes with extra room in the front of the shoe. There are shoes available that do have extra width and depth. Your shoe salesperson can assist you with finding the shoe that is right for you.

Painful feet are a common reason people don't walk as far or as often as they used to. Supportive, properly fitted footwear can make a difference in your ability to walk safely and comfortably.

Wheelchairs and Electric Carts

For people who are unable to walk because of paralysis, weakened muscles, poor lung capacity, unstable or unsafe gait, or amputation, a wheelchair or electric cart may be the safest method of mobility. The type of chair that is best for you and your problems should be determined by a qualified professional. Unwarranted use of a wheelchair can lead to dependency on the wheelchair, weakened muscles, decreased endurance, and decreased mobility.

Wheelchairs and carts are available from several manufacturers and have a variety of options, such as seating surfaces, armrests, backrests, leg rests, and controls. The cost of a wheelchair varies depending whether it is a standard chair, an electric chair, or is equipped with other options. It is in your best interest to contact a qualified professional, such as a physical or occupational therapist, to determine your needs and to help you order the chair. A customized wheelchair (and cushion) should be purchased if you will be sitting in it for more than 2 hours per day. This will prevent the development of skin ulcers and spinal deformities.

Considerations When Ordering a Wheelchair or Cart

Following are some issues you need to consider when ordering a wheelchair.

1. How many hours per day will you sit in the chair? Will it be used mainly for transporting?

2. Will you be using the chair in your home only, or will you use it outdoors?

3. How will you propel the chair? Will you use your arms or your legs, or will someone be pushing you?

4. What are the widths of the doorways in your home? Will the chair fit into the bedroom, the bathroom, and so on.

5. Is your skin healthy? Will you require a special cushion for the chair?

6. Who will pay for the wheelchair? Medicare, Medicaid, or private insurance will pay for a wheelchair only if it is deemed medically necessary by your physician, or if it will improve your functional abilities.

There are other issues that the qualified professional will address and specific measurements that must be taken to ensure a good match between you and your wheelchair.

Ramps

If you are no longer able to walk up the stairs to your home because you are using a rolling walker or in a wheelchair, you may need to build a ramp to enter your home.

If you have family members with experience in construction, they may be able to build the ramp; or you may need to contact a contractor to do the work. Some prefabricated ramps can be purchased through adaptive equipment catalogs.

You may need to obtain a building permit to construct a ramp. Each city has ordinances for building permits. You will need to contact your local city planning and development department to learn the specifics.

If you build your own ramp, there are certain specifications that are required for independent and safe use. These specifications are listed below (see the pictures on p. 125).

Ramp Specifications

1. Ramps must be at least 3 feet 6 inches wide. A width of 5 feet is preferred for walkways to accommodate the wheelchair turning radius.

2. Ramps must be of a nonslip material, yet the finish should not be so rough as to make the wheelchair travel difficult or unpleasant.

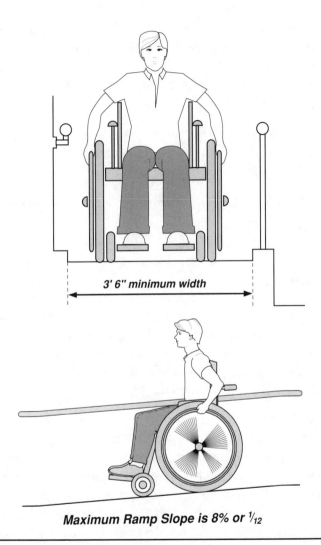

3' 6" minimum width

Maximum Ramp Slope is 8% or ¹/₁₂

The maximum allowable gradient for a ramp is 8 percent (1-inch rise for 12-inch length). The minimum width of a ramp is 42 inches wide.

3. Ramps must not exceed an 8 percent slope (no greater than a 1-inch rise for every 12 inches of length). If the slope exceeds 5 percent, however, handrails on both sides may be necessary for the individual to propel him- or herself.

4. Ramps typically constitute a means of emergency exit and, therefore, must be of fire-retardant construction.

5. A low curb (approximately 4 inches high) on one or both sides of a ramp will serve as a guardrail for the wheelchair.

Summary

Many older adults are at substantial risk of falling because of intrinsic and environmental factors. Because the home is the most common location of falls, it is in your best interest to take a close look at your home and make changes now, before an accident happens.

Resources are available to help you identify and implement the necessary changes, including people such as your physician, physical therapist, occupational therapist, architect, or contractor. If your physician is unable to provide a referral, you can contact most of these professionals by looking through the yellow pages of your phone book under specific headings or under the general heading of Senior Citizens' Services. You may also contact your local commission on aging for information. Your local medical supply distributor or pharmacy will have information regarding the availability and cost of adaptive equipment. Do not hesitate to contact such resources. Making changes to reduce your risks of falls may also allow you to live in your home longer—something most of us want to do.

References

Some information in this chapter was adapted from the following sources:

Robinson, M. B. (no date). *Equipment and suggestions to help the patient with Parkinson's disease in the activities of daily living.* (Booklet available from the American Parkinson's Disease Association, Inc.)

Tideikksaar, Rein. (1989). Geriatric falls: Assessing the cause, preventing recurrence. *Geriatrics, 44,* 57–64.

Chapter 9

Sexual Expression

Sexual expression is often not discussed at all, but is important during aging and illness. Sexuality is an important part of who you are and affects how you feel about yourself. This chapter will review normal sexual functioning and myths and realities regarding sexual dysfunction.

Aging and Sex

Sexual expression and feeling are normal at any age. Sexual interest is healthy and to be expected in old age. Many people inappropriately assume that older adults will not express sexuality. Even some health professionals may communicate this idea. In the United States today, the possibility of sexually transmitted disease should be discussed for adults of all ages, particularly when starting a new relationship.

Negative and harmful stereotypes include the "dirty old man" and the "prudish older female." These stereotypes are inaccurate and create barriers to normal sexual expression. People tend to focus on sexual intercourse as the only sexual behavior. Sexual behavior is quite varied and includes smiling, flirting, holding hands, hugging, kissing, and feeling an attachment to another.

There are several components to sexuality aside from reproductive function. The major components are sensuality and intimacy. Sensuality is the reaction to one's own or to another's body, the need to be touched. This does not have to be genital touch. Holding hands may suffice where other sexual contact is not possible. Some women have been raised to believe they have few sensual pleasure rights. The current sexual climate in the United States is much more open, but this does not mean you will want or be able to change the way you feel as a result of your upbringing.

Intimacy is the emotional counterpart to sensuality, a closeness or openness to another person. Both intimacy and sensuality may be lost for the widow or widower. This loss also can occur during hospitalization or during a nursing home stay. Many people give up the opportunity for intimacy by ignoring or denying their feelings. You must acknowledge and explore your own needs for intimacy and sensuality and recognize that these needs are normal and healthy.

Changes in the Physiology of Intercourse During Aging

There are physiological changes in sexual function with advancing age. The four stages of sexual physiology— excitement, plateau, orgasm, and resolution—are all affected.

Excitement takes longer for both genders. Erection or lubrication occurs after several minutes or longer of stimulation. The plateau phase of sexual tension tends to last longer in the older adult. If penetration is painful for the female, it may be due to vaginal changes, abstinence, or bladder or urethral inflammation. All painful situations should be discussed with a knowledgeable physician. Use of a water-soluble lubricant may help if the vagina is dry. These are available in drug stores without prescription. Orgasm may not occur in either gender. Emission of seminal fluid in the older man is less than in younger men. If uterine contractions during the female orgasm are spastic and painful, medical consultation is indicated. Resolution occurs more rapidly in the older adult of both genders. Older males will not be able to have an erection for several hours after orgasm.

Recognition of the physiologic changes in sexual function with advancing age is important. These changes are gradual and not related to disease. If you note difficulty or change in sexual function that exceeds the changes described, consult with a knowledgeable physician or reputable counselor.

Factors That Affect Sexual Expression

People who are active sexually tend to remain active as they age, although sexual activity may decline somewhat after age 70. Unavailability of a partner and poor health certainly contribute to this decline.

Alcohol is touted as an aphrodisiac; however, it can interfere with a man's potency. Smoking causes more rapid aging of the sex organs in both men and women. Fear of acquiring a sexually transmitted disease, like the human immune deficiency virus, may interfere with the ability to form relationships.

Surgery

Surgery also can affect sexual function. Removal of a breast may leave a woman feeling unattractive. After surgery on the prostate gland, some men will not be able to sustain an erection. Surgery on the prostate gland can lead to urinary incontinence, which may be seen as unattractive. After prostate surgery, men may experience retrograde ejaculation. This means that semen is ejaculated into the bladder and does not come out of the penis except during urination. Surgery on the intestines resulting in an external appliance like an ostomy bag may interfere with sexual function because of odor, appearance, or doubt about self-image or the capacity for intimacy. A hip or knee replacement operation can make a partner shy or afraid of hurting you. Nonetheless, none of these operations necessarily causes a decline in desire for sexual expression nor should they make sexual satisfaction unattainable.

Medical Illness

The amount of energy needed for sexual intercourse is similar to climbing a flight of stairs. If you have the energy for one, you the have the energy needed for the other. Even if you cannot climb a flight of stairs, you can still be active sexually. Sex early in the day is recommended for cardiac patients and for others who become fatigued over the course of the day. Arthritis patients may benefit from taking aspirin or other pain medication before sexual intimacy. People with arthritis may need the assistance of a properly placed pillow to support themselves. A side-by-side position may be more comfortable and least exerting for both parties. After an operation or a heart attack, sexual activity should be resumed gradually. Sitting in a chair with one partner on the other's lap can be less exerting for the partner on the bottom.

Medications

Prescription medications can cause sexual problems for both men and women. Men may experience inhibited ejaculation, difficulty with erections, enlarged breasts, or shrinkage of the testicles. Women may have low sex drive, trouble with orgasm, or decreased lubrication.

Almost any medication can cause sexual problems, but this side effect does not occur for all people taking a particular medicine. Water pills (diuretics), blood-pressure medicines, heart medicines, ulcer medications, anticholinergics or antihistamines found in common cold remedies, sedatives, tranquilizers, and antidepressant medicines can all cause sexual problems.

Many physicians are undereducated about the problems that medications can cause to sexuality. Don't be afraid to ask your doctor or pharmacist if a medication you take might interfere with your sexual function. In addition, look for nonmedicine remedies for controlling disease (see Chapter 3). When starting a new medicine, or when you have reason for concern regarding sexual performance, ask to see the package insert for medicines you are taking or similar information from the *Physicians' Desk Reference*. Your doctor or pharmacist can help interpret this information. If necessary, get a second opinion about the medications you are taking. Remember that it could be dangerous to stop a medication without your physician's advice.

Summary

Problems can arise in sexual relationships because of aging or disease. To solve these problems you need communication between partners. When it comes to intimacy, you must be honest. Humor and openness about desires, abilities, and expectations are also important. Creativity in sexual expression takes two people.

Good planning can be helpful to help get away from other concerns and focus on your romantic relationship. Range of motion exercises before sexual activity may help to limber you. Relaxation techniques like deep-breathing or guided imagery may be helpful. Counseling also may be helpful to your relationship.

Above all focus on your strengths, not your limitations. You are not less attractive or less sexy to those who care about you simply because of your illness or aging.

References

Some information in this chapter was adapted from the following sources.

Buchholz, B. B., & Hayes, J. (1992, May-June). Keeping sex alive. *Arthritis Today*, 34–38.

Crenshaw, T. L. (1992, January-February). Sexual problems by prescription. *Saturday Evening Post*, 64–69.

Scheingold, L. D., & Wagner, N. W. (1974). *Sound sex and the aging heart*. New York: Human Sciences.

Chapter 10

Housing Options
as You Age

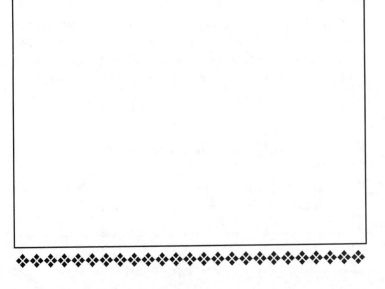

Housing arrangements are important at every stage of your life. Fortunately, there are many housing alternatives available to you as you age. This chapter is designed to help you look at your noninstitutional housing needs and to understand the options you have to meet those needs. Nursing homes also provide housing for older people who need an institutional setting, and this will be discussed in Chapter 11.

Why People Resist Changing Housing Arrangements

Most older people want to remain in their own homes as they age. They may have lived in a particular location for many years and feel comfortable with their neighbors and neighborhood. Cost also may be a factor. Often, older people have paid for their homes and don't want to make monthly payments for housing again. People frequently feel an emotional closeness to a home where they have lived for many years. They have probably raised their children in that home and have many pleasant memories. Perhaps they have modified the home to meet their needs by installing an outside ramp or grab bars in the bathroom, and they feel secure in the environment. An older person also may view giving up a home as a sign that he or she is less independent and less capable.

Reasons to Consider Relocation

There are good reasons for some older people to consider relocation. Declining or poor health is often the primary reason to relocate. A person in poor health often has difficulty maintaining a residence. The outdoor work as well as the indoor upkeep of a home may become more than the older person can handle. Another reason to relocate may be that services such as help with meals and housekeeping are needed on a more consistent basis. Sometimes the loss of a driver's license can precipitate relocation especially if transportation resources are scarce. The death of a spouse and increased social isolation can also contribute to relocation. Some older people decide to leave their neighborhoods when crime becomes an issue. An apartment with the security of more neighbors, an intercom system, a resident manager, and/or limited access to the building via a security door or doorman may be attractive to these individuals.

Staying in Your Own Home

If you choose to remain in your own home, some assistance may help increase the length of time you can remain at home. For example, help with housekeeping and yard work can make life easier for you as you age. If you have health problems, you may need additional help such as personal care, meal preparation, or nursing care. Some older people find that relatives or neighbors are willing to provide help on a regular basis. Often, spouses and/or adult children take on caregiving roles for their loved ones when they need more help. Most people look to these informal sources of support before exploring options available in the community. However, there are times when more formal support from a community agency can help you maintain your independent lifestyle.

Community Resources for Help at Home

You may need help from a community agency when your needs exceed both your capabilities and the resources you have available. For example, you may need help with a bath or with housekeeping or home maintenance. You may, because of illness or disability, be unable to cook for yourself or manage your own shopping. Obtaining the help you need will increase the likelihood that you will be able to remain in your own home in spite of disability. The following list provides you with information about where to look when you need this kind of help.

Information and Referral Service

Many communities operate a telephone hotline to help you find agencies that offer the services you need. These Information and Referral hotline telephone numbers can be found in the yellow pages of the phone book under "Information Bureaus."

Eldercare Locator

The Eldercare Locator is a hotline sponsored by the National Association of Area Agencies on Aging that can provide you with the phone numbers of local agencies that provide services to older people. The hotline number (1-800-677-1116) is operational from 9:00 a.m. to 7:00 p.m. Eastern Time.

State and County Aging Agencies

In 1965, the federal Older Americans Act allocated funds to provide services to seniors and their caregivers. The

State Bureau on Aging (or state agency with a similar name) is responsible for legislated state and federal Older Americans Act funds and for development of a coordinated, comprehensive system of services to older people. The Area Agency on Aging allocates Older Americans Act funds to counties in its district and provides direct technical assistance to those counties. Then, there are the county aging units that receive and administer the Older Americans Act and state funds that are allocated for local programs and services. Some examples of these services are: congregate and home-delivered meals, transportation, outreach services, individual and family counseling, telephone reassurance, friendly visiting, and senior centers. The county aging unit may be called the County Aging Program or other appropriate name in your area. Check the state and county government listings in the phone book for the phone numbers of these agencies.

Personal Care

A nurse and/or other health professional(s) can visit you in your home if your physician feels that you need home care services. Home health agencies are listed in the yellow pages of the phone book under "Nurses." Most agencies can provide physical therapy, medical social work services, and personal care (for example, an attendant to help with bathing). If you need skilled services (services that can only be provided by skilled professionals such as nurses or physical therapists), then Medicare and your private insurance supplement may provide reimbursement. If the services you need are not considered to be skilled, then you will probably have to pay privately for this assistance.

Chore Help

If you need help with housekeeping, cooking, or home maintenance, you should consider hiring a chore worker. Some community agencies provide this service for older people and charge them according to ability to pay. Your local County Aging Unit (or other aging coalition) or Department of Social Services may be able to help you locate an agency to help you. These offices are listed in the county government listings in the phone book. A local senior center may also be a resource for you. The senior center Director should be able to help you find an agency that can meet your needs.

Nutrition

Most areas have a "Meals on Wheels" program to provide daily noon meals to disabled and/or homebound persons. Home-delivered meals provide one nutritious meal five to seven times per week if you are unable to handle your own cooking. Generally, a doctor's order is needed to specify the diet required. Nutrition sites are also a resource if you are not homebound. These sites often are located at senior centers and offer an opportunity for socialization as well as a nutritious meal.

Transportation

Many communities have resources for rides to meal sites, medical appointments, and shopping areas. Cities with mass transit will more than likely provide special vehicles to transport handicapped individuals. This service can be found by looking in the city government listings of the phone book. In some areas, private companies provide handicapped transportation services. Look in the yellow pages of the phone book under "Transportation Service for Disabled" or "Ambulance Service."

Friendly Visitors/Telephone Reassurance

A regular visitor or telephone caller can be an important resource for some individuals. These visitors are part of Reassurance Programs sponsored by different agencies or community groups (social service agencies, churches, aging coalitions, and so on). Usually these volunteers visit on a regular basis to provide companionship or help with simple tasks such as letter writing. If you live alone, a friendly visitor can become an important part of your weekly routine. A reassurance phone call (where a caller checks on you) on a regular basis can increase your feelings of security at home. These programs can be found by contacting your local "Information and Referral Service," county social service office, or county aging unit.

Emergency Response System

This program is designed to allow you to call for help if you are injured or ill and cannot get to the telephone. Emergency Response Systems are usually sponsored by a hospital. Typically, you wear a necklace or bracelet that has a button to push in case help is needed. When you push the button, a central receiving station (such as a hospital) is alerted to your distress. An operator will call to check on you. If you can't be reached, the operator will call someone you have identified as a responder and ask that person to check on you. Emergency help will be sent if no one can be reached or if you or your responder indicates that help is needed. This type of device provides security for you if you have health conditions and especially if you live alone. You can obtain information on emergency response by calling your local "Information and Referral Service" or a local hospital.

Respite

If you feel that you need a break from the demands of providing care for another person, respite programs are available in many communities. Respite can be provided either by in-home caregivers for a few hours at a time, by an adult day care center that provides a program of appropriate structured activity and health services 1 to 5 days per week, or by admission to a nursing home for a short stay. All of these services are designed to give the person providing care (caregiver) some needed time away from caregiving. You can learn about the respite resources available in your community by contacting the Information and Referral service in your area or by contacting your local county Department of Social Services, County Aging Unit, or the Social Work Department at a local hospital.

Home Adaptations

If you are disabled, home adaptations designed to help modify the environment to meet your needs can help you remain at home. Examples are ramps for wheelchair access to the house and bathroom modifications. Home health agencies, occupational therapists, or nonprofit design groups often can help arrange for you to adapt your home to meet your needs. Look in the yellow pages of the phone book under "Nurses," "Occupational Therapists," or for a nonprofit design agency under "Architects." Chapter 8 of this book contains more detailed information on home adaptations that may interest you.

Changing Your Housing Arrangement

At some point, you may decide that a different housing arrangement would benefit you. Some of the options that may be available in your community are discussed below.

Homesharing

This is an arrangement where you share your home in exchange for help with the expenses or chores that you are no longer capable of managing independently. Each person has his or her own bedroom but shares common areas such as the living room, dining room, kitchen, and so forth. Some community agencies help match homeowners with people interested in such an arrangement. Contact your local Information and Referral telephone hotline or your local County Department of Social Services or Human Services office for assistance in finding a homeshare program.

Advantages of Homesharing

Homesharing is economical. It also provides assistance that may allow you remain at home instead of relocating to an apartment. You may find that you enjoy the companionship of living with another person, and you may feel more secure than if you lived alone.

Disadvantages of Homesharing

There is an inevitable loss of privacy, and the arrangement may not work because of interpersonal conflict. Zoning restrictions may be an issue in some locations.

Accessory Apartment

This is an arrangement where a self-contained apartment is built onto an existing home. You continue to live independently whether the unit is added to your home and rented to another person, or a relative or friend builds the unit in his or her home for you to occupy. Contact a builder or contractor in your area for an estimate on the cost. If you decide to build the accessory apartment, it is wise to contact several builders for competitive bids.

Advantages of an Accessory Apartment

There is an increased resale value of the home for the homeowner. Also, there exists the possibility of an exchange of services between the two parties.

Disadvantages of an Accessory Apartment

The cost is the primary disadvantage to this type of housing arrangement. Construction of an additional apartment unit can be expensive and, of course, property taxes will increase as the value of the home increases. Another consideration relates to the zoning laws. Some neighborhoods may not allow this kind of construction to a single family home.

ECHO Housing

ECHO stands for Elder Cottage Housing Opportunity. An ECHO home is a small cottage that is placed in the yard of a single family home. This enables an older person to live close to family while maintaining a separate household. Check the yellow pages of the phone book under "Manufactured Housing" or "Mobile Homes—Dealers" to inquire about the purchase of a unit that you could use as ECHO housing if this housing arrangement interests you.

Advantages of ECHO Housing

Typically, this type of housing is economical, and the units are designed specifically to meet the needs of older adults, that is, barrier free. Obviously, this type of housing is an advantage for the person who desires privacy and autonomy yet seeks the security of living close to family if assistance is needed.

Disadvantages of ECHO Housing

The unit probably will be small and may not work well on small property lots. As in the accessory apartment, zoning restrictions may be an issue. For this reason, ECHO housing is not common in the United States.

Senior Citizen Apartments

Typically, these apartments are subsidized by the federal government and are found in most areas. Rent is based on a percentage of a person's income. These apartments can be located by contacting your local Housing Authority listed in the county government listings in the phone book.

Advantages of Senior Citizen Apartments

The cost is low, and the apartment provides for an increased feeling of security (some buildings maintain security systems). This arrangement also provides for companionship possibilities because most residents become acquainted with their neighbors. Additionally, some apartment complexes offer services.

Disadvantages of Senior Citizen Apartments

The main disadvantage for some people is the age segregation. Some people prefer to live close to people of various ages, including children. Others may be quite content to live close to older adults only.

Congregate Housing

This type of housing for older people provides services and staff to administer programs. The service most often provided is a meal program. Other services available at some sites include housekeeping, transportation, and social activities. As with subsidized apartments, you can locate congregate housing by contacting your local Housing Authority.

Advantages of Congregate Housing

The advantages of congregate housing include the services just mentioned as well as the possibility of a government subsidy for rent. There also are opportunities for companionship and friendship offered by this type of housing arrangement.

Disadvantages of Congregate Housing

Some people consider the age segregation to be a disadvantage. Likewise, some people may not be interested in the group dining and services offered.

Board and Care Homes

These facilities are called by different names in different localities. Other common terms are Community Based Residential Facility, Residential Care Facility, and Assisted Living Facility. Typically, a Board and Care Home has 24-hour staff coverage to provide help with chores such as meals, laundry, and housekeeping. The cost of these services is included in the rent charges. Some facilities offer additional assistance such as help with medication management and personal care (bathing, dressing, and similar tasks). Some Board and Care Homes offer activities and outings to increase socialization. Most offer a home-like setting with shared community areas such as TV rooms, sitting rooms, and a dining area. Often, bathroom space is shared as well. Many states require these facilities to be licensed. This helps to ensure that fire, safety, and health standards are met. Licensing requirements also may ensure 24-hour staff coverage. If you are interested in such a housing arrangement, you should tour the facility and ask questions about the day-to-day operation. You also could contact the state licensing agency to obtain information about how well the facility fared in its last inspection. These facilities can be found in the yellow pages of the phone book under "Retirement & Life Care Communities and Homes."

Advantages of Board and Care Homes

The main advantage of a Board and Care home is that it provides a means of preserving autonomy as your ability to perform self-care decreases. It provides a safe environment with services yet allows you to come and go as you please. The atmosphere is more home-like, less institutional, and less restrictive than a nursing home.

Disadvantages of Board and Care Homes

Board and Care Homes offer less privacy than living independently. As in any group living arrangement, the risk of interpersonal conflict with a roommate or other residents exists. Private rooms are not always available and are more costly than semiprivate rooms. You will need to consider how you feel about a roommate and living in a group situation. Another disadvantage may relate to the cost. Board and Care facilities are not covered by Medicare or Medical Assistance programs. The cost is more than elderly housing apartments because of the services offered. One other disadvantage is that some facilities are not barrier-free. For example, the facility may have stairs and no elevator or doorways may not be large enough to accommodate a wheelchair. Therefore, you may have to relocate if your ability to ambulate changes.

Retirement Communities

A retirement community is a housing arrangement that provides at least minimal services for retired older people. Retirement communities can be separate communities or a center composed of apartments and other levels of housing.

Separate Communities for Retirement

Retirement communities that are separate communities are called Retirement New Towns, Villages, and Subdivisions. A good example of a Retirement New Town is Sun City, Arizona. People move to Sun City to retire and must be a certain age to buy property. Typically, a *Retirement New Town* is developed privately and marketed to young, active retirees. Services such as health care are available as well as commercial development for shopping, banking, leisure, and recreation. A *Retirement Village* is similar to a New Town except it is a more medium-size community. It provides recreation and leisure resources but typically is less commercially developed and less likely to provide health care services. A *Retirement Subdivision* is smaller yet and has limited recreation resources. Typically, health care services and commercial development do not exist in these communities. Residents tend to be young retirees in good health who receive their health care in neighboring communities.

Housing Complexes for Retirement

Another type of retirement community is characterized by a complex of housing units that offer services. The *Retirement Residence* is one such example. In this type of housing arrangement, services and programs are provided to facilitate an independent lifestyle with individual and group activities available on the premises. Outdoor recreation services usually are not part of the residence. These facilities are likely to be developed by nonprofit sponsors such as churches or fraternal orders. Sometimes the residence is developed with the use of federal assistance programs and thus is able to offer units to accommodate low to moderate income retirees. Residents of these facilities typically are older retirees with few serious health problems.

Another retirement community in this category is the *Continuing Care Retirement Center (CCRC)*. This common type of retirement community offers health care for residents as their needs change. Typically, the Continuing Care Retirement Center provides retirement apartments with an optional meal program. Assistance with housekeeping and personal care can usually be arranged by the staff of the facility, which typically includes an apartment manager and a nurse and perhaps a social worker. Also located on the grounds of the CCRC is a nursing home that can provide rehabilitation, temporary care, or nursing home care on a long-term basis. Often, Continuing Care Retirement Centers are sponsored by nonprofit organizations such as religious denominations. However, private, for-profit centers also exist. The advantage of a CCRC is the continuity provided by a less radical relocation if your needs change. Also, most residents feel more secure in an environment where staff are available to respond in case of an emergency and to help make arrangements if more care is needed. Residents of CCRCs tend to be older than residents of other retirement communities.

Yet another type of housing development may be even more common for retirement living: the *Naturally Occurring Retirement Community or NORC*. This housing development is not planned or designed for older people but, over time, it has become populated by mostly older residents. The NORC may be a neighborhood or an apartment complex or building. The fact that these communities typically are located close to services has contributed to their popularity with older adults. They are age integrated since they are not specifically built for older people. However, they offer the companionship opportunities of elderly housing units because more than 50 percent of the residents are older. The advantages of a Naturally Occurring Retirement Community include the proximity to services and the companionship possibilities. Many NORC apartment complexes provide security doors and other safety measures that are attractive to older residents. The disadvantage of a NORC is that you may have to relocate if your health needs change and in-home services are inadequate. However, most people in any housing arrangement (except the Continuing Care Retirement Center) will be faced with this possibility if they need residential or nursing home care.

Advantages and Disadvantages to Retirement Community Living

Living in any type of retirement community has advantages and disadvantages that will, of course, be based on your preferences and needs during retirement. Only you can decide if retirement community living is what you want. Some of the common advantages and disadvantages are listed below.

Advantages. A retirement community offers services and facilities that can make your retirement more enjoyable. It also offers a setting where you can make new friends who have mutual interests. Retirement communities promote an active lifestyle that is based on your ability to participate. The activities of a Retirement New Town will be different from those of the Continuing Care Retirement Communities because of the age and health status of residents found in these types of retirement communities. Nevertheless, the activities offered in both settings encourage the resident to be as active as possible during the retirement years.

Disadvantages. Age segregation may be an issue. Some people prefer living close to age peers and others prefer living in proximity to people of different ages. Cost also may be an issue. Low income individuals will not be able to afford some retirement communities. However, you may be able to obtain a rent subsidy at some facilities if your income meets guidelines. For those who prefer the age integration, the Naturally Occurring Retirement Community offers a retirement-type setting with services close by.

The picture on page 156 shows many of the housing options and services discussed in this chapter.

Summary

A continuum of interesting community-based housing options exists for older adults that range from residential to assisted-living facilities. However, there is no formula for determining what is the best option for you. You need to examine your own situation to determine the best fit between your needs and the type of environment best suited to meet those needs. This type of planning allows you to maintain maximum independence for as long as possible.

References

Some information in this chapter was adapted from the following sources.

American Association of Retired Persons in Cooperation with the Federal Trade Commission. (1985). *Your home, your choice: A workbook for older people and their families*. Washington, DC: American Association of Retired Persons.

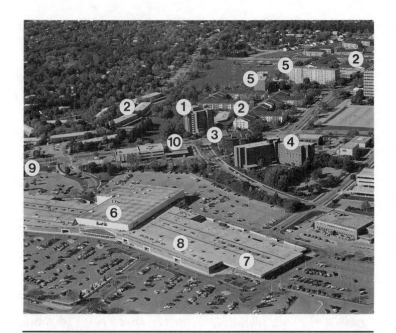

Neighborhood with Elderly Housing and Services: 1. Planned Retirement Community; 2. NORC Apartments; 3. NORC Condominium; 4. Subsidized Housing for Elderly; 5. Non-NORC Apartments; 6. Shopping Center; 7. Grocery store; 8. Pharmacy; 9. Bank; and 10. Post Office

Hunt, M. E., Feldt, A. G., Marans, R. W., Pastalan, L. A., & Vakalo, K. L. (1983). *Retirement communities: An American original.* New York: The Haworth Press.

Hunt, M. E., & Gunter-Hunt, G. (1983). Simulated site visits in the relocation of older people. *Health and Social Work, 8,* 5–14.

Hunt, M. E., & Gunter-Hunt, G. (1985). Naturally Occurring Retirement Communities. *Journal of Housing for the Elderly, 3,* 3–21.

Hunt, M. E. (no date). *Naturally Occurring Retirement Communities* (brochure available from AARP Andrus Foundation, 1901 K Street, NW, Washington DC 20049).

Chapter 11

Nursing Homes

A nursing home may be the best option if you need 24-hour nursing care that is not practical or financially possible to receive at home. This chapter provides information that can help you plan for nursing home care if you need it.

A nursing home (or nursing facility) offers skilled nursing care and rehabilitation services as well as regular health-related services that can be available only through an institutional facility. The term "skilled care" means that the care provided requires the services of trained nurses or other professionals. This level of care must be above the room and board level and is not intended for the care management of persons with mental illness.

All nursing homes must be licensed and are required by law to have a Medical Director and licensed nursing personnel. The facility must screen all admissions for a diagnosis of serious mental illness and/or mental retardation. Patients with these diagnoses (serious mental illness or mental retardation) must be evaluated by the state to determine their need for nursing home care and for specialized services related to their diagnoses. Those individuals found not to need nursing home care or specialized services may not be admitted to the facility. All patients who are appropriate for admission must receive a comprehensive assessment by the nursing home staff within 14 days of admission. Reassessments must be conducted when a resident's physical or mental condition changes significantly and at least once a year thereafter. The facility must develop a plan of care to organize services and activities for each resident with the goal of achieving the highest physical, mental, and psychosocial well-being that is practical for that person.

The services typically provided in nursing homes include licensed nurses around the clock, an activities program, and in larger facilities rehabilitative services and social work services. Resident councils are a means for residents to express concerns about policies or procedures and to feel they have some say in the way the facility is governed. Residents have the right to express grievances and to receive a prompt response to a grievance.

Payment

Nursing home care can be costly. If you are considering admission to a nursing home, you undoubtedly will be concerned about how your care will be financed. People often mistakenly assume that Medicare will cover any nursing home stay. Unfortunately, this is not the case. Therefore, you will want to know your options if you need nursing home care. (Also see Chapter 13.)

Medicare

Medicare provides limited coverage for nursing home care. The following criteria must be met for Medicare payment:

1. You must choose a Medicare-certified nursing home. Since all nursing homes are not Medicare certified, you will want to ask the facility representative about this certification.

2. You must be assigned a Medicare-certified bed. This means that the nursing home may have a bed avail-

able, but it must be one of their designated Medicare beds for Medicare to pay for your stay.

3. The nursing home must file a Medicare claim for you.

4. You must have been hospitalized for 3 days prior to your admission and that hospitalization must have been within the past 30 days.

5. You must be receiving treatment in the nursing home for a condition that was treated in the hospital or that developed in the hospital.

6. You must be in need of skilled care on a daily basis (with certain exceptions), and you must need to receive this care in a nursing home.

As you can see, these guidelines are quite restrictive. Even when Medicare does provide coverage, the number of days for the coverage is limited. Clearly, Medicare is not a resource for long-term nursing home care payment.

Medicare Supplemental Insurance

These policies, also called medigap insurance, address the gaps in cost coverage of Medicare. Generally, supplemental policies provide coverage for a service if it is approved by Medicare. No coverage is available for those services that Medicare does not cover at least partially. You will need to read your policy to determine if it will pay the co-pay for a nursing home stay after Medicare coverage in full expires. If so, this would increase the number of days available to you at no cost. However, supplemental insurance is, like Medicare, generally not a resource if you need long-term nursing home care.

Nursing Home Insurance

Typically, nursing home insurance policies pay you a certain amount of money for each day that you receive nursing home care. You should read the policy carefully and make sure you understand any restrictions before purchasing this type of insurance from an insurance company. The availability of this kind of insurance may vary in different locations.

Medical Assistance, Medicaid or Title 19

This is a joint state-federal health benefits program based on financial need. In other words, Medical Assistance is a program for people with very low income and resources.

The guidelines for qualifying financially and the benefits paid by the Medical Assistance program to a beneficiary vary from state to state. To qualify for Medical Assistance to pay for nursing home care, you must meet financial criteria as well as medical criteria. The medical criteria guidelines are determined by each state participating in the program. Most states also have provisions that deny medical assistance benefits to any individual who gives away or transfers property, money, or other assets (called divestment) within a certain number of years before applying for the program. In some states there are exceptions to these divestment laws. For example, your state law may allow you to leave a homestead to a minor child or a developmentally disabled child living in it. A spouse is typically exempt from divestment provisions.

It is important to note that provisions are made to protect a nursing home resident's spouse (who is living in the community) from impoverishment. Generally, spouses are allowed to keep a certain amount of income and assets. These maximum amounts vary from state to state. However, the community-dwelling spouse generally will be able to keep enough income to meet his or her basic needs and will be able to maintain some personal savings as well.

Private Pay

If you don't qualify for Medicare or Medical Assistance coverage and you have no insurance to help with the cost of nursing home care, you will be faced with paying privately for your care. In many instances, individuals spend down their resources until they qualify for Medical Assistance coverage.

What to Look For

When you consider a nursing home, you'll want to find a facility that meets your needs medically and socially. The best way to make that happen is advance planning before a crisis. It would be to your advantage if you knew something about nursing homes in your area in case you need to be admitted. You will want to consider location and the level of care that each facility can provide. It will be easier for your family and friends to visit if you reside in a local facility. You also may want to call the state Department of Health (or other appropriate licensing agency) to determine how well certain facilities fared in their last inspections. Some of the information that you want can be obtained by a telephone call to the nursing home administrator. Once you have screened nursing homes initially in this way, then you can decide which facilities to visit.

Information from a Screening Phone Call

1. What kind of care does the nursing home provide? Some examples of care you may need are: skilled care (care that requires trained nurses or other professionals, for example, help with bandage changes or tube feedings); rehabilitative care (treatment by an occupational, physical, or speech therapist to restore function); convalescent care (necessary treatment and help with personal care while you recover from a major illness or surgery).

2. What are the possibilities for financial arrangements? Does the facility accept Medical Assistance? Is the facility Medicare certified? Does the facility have a contract with the Department of Veterans Affairs to provide care for eligible veterans? What are the billing arrangements? Is a deposit required?

3. How large is the facility?

4. Are physical, occupational, and speech therapy services provided? Which physicians make visits?

5. What types of activities are offered?

6. Can you bring personal belongings with you?

7. What is the staff to resident ratio?

8. Is there a resident council?

9. Are beds usually available or does the facility have a waiting list?

10. What is the cost per day for each level of care?

Once you have determined which facilities have the amenities that interest you, plan to tour these nursing homes. Schedule the tour on a day when you have plenty of time. You will want to ask lots of questions, and you should stay long enough to get a "feel" for how content the residents are and how attentive the staff is. The following checklist will help you obtain relevant information during your tour.

Checklist for a Nursing Home Tour

1. *Observe the residents.* Are the residents out of bed, dressed, clean, and well groomed? Do the residents appear alert? Do they seem over-medicated? Are the residents busy? Do the residents seem comfortable? Are they engaged in socializing with each other?

2. *Observe the staff.* What is the general mood of the staff? Are they friendly and courteous? Does the staff (including the administrative staff) know the residents by their names? Does the staff seem to respect privacy? Does the staff respond to calls for assistance in a timely manner? What is the resident to nursing staff ratio? What other health care professionals are available at this facility (such as occupational therapy, physical therapy, and social work). Is there adequate staff to help you plan for discharge if you are able to return to the community? Is there a regular inservice training program for the staff?

3. *Observe the physical aspects of the facility.* How clean is the overall facility? Do you notice odors? Is the facility well lighted? Are the hallways free of obstacles? Does the temperature seem appropriate for the time of year? Are fire exits and fire extinguishers visible?

Rooms. Are the resident rooms attractively furnished? Have residents brought any of their own furniture, bedding, or pictures or otherwise decorated their rooms? Does the closet space seem adequate? How many residents occupy each room? Are private rooms available?

Bathrooms. Are the bathrooms conveniently located? How many residents share each bathroom? Is there a separate area for bathing? Is there a whirlpool?

Common areas. How many lounge areas are available? Are they adequately furnished? Is the lounge space adequate for the number of residents? Is the dining room attractively furnished and accessible? How many residents eat there at any one time? Does mealtime seem enjoyable or hectic? Is a weekly menu posted? Is a variety of food offered? Is smoking allowed in common areas? If so, how are the needs of nonsmokers accommodated? If not, is alternate smoking space available?

Activity areas. How many activity areas are available? Are they adequately furnished to accommodate various activities? Is there a posted schedule of activities ? Are the activities varied so as to appeal to many residents? Are activities planned outside of the facility? Are activities available for residents with different disabilities? Are families included in any of the activities?

Specialized service areas. Is there a nondenominational chapel or other area for worship or meditation? Are other specialized areas available, such as a therapy room for occupational or physical therapy, a beauty or barber shop, an area in which to talk privately with a staff person or family members? Are these areas adequately furnished or equipped?

4. *Miscellaneous observations.* Is the facility licensed? Is the license available for you to review? Is there a Resident's Council? If so, how often does it meet? Is there a policy for filing a complaint? Is there an open-door visitation policy or specific visiting hours? What is the smoking policy in the nursing home? Are telephones available for resident use (telephone jacks for those who want a private phone and public telephones elsewhere in the facility)? How will your privacy be protected? What are your rights as a resident?

Because this is a lot of information to obtain, you may want to make second visits to the facilities that interest you the most, perhaps unannounced. It also is a good idea to ask friends and relatives if they know of anyone who has lived at the nursing home you are considering. Perhaps talking with that person or his or her relatives will help you gain information about the quality of care provided. You also could ask your physician and minister for their opinions if they have visited patients or parishioners there. A nursing home's good reputation is usually well deserved.

Relocation Stress

Relocation can be stressful, especially if it is not voluntary. The move to a nursing home signifies a change in functioning that most people hope will never happen to them. This is not usually a move that people look forward to as they might a move to a retirement setting. However, it is a move that sometimes has to occur.

The stress of making this kind of move can be addressed by making yourself as familiar with your new environment as possible before you actually move in. By learning "the lay of the land," you will be taking control of those aspects of the move that are possible to control. As mentioned earlier in this chapter, you should visit the facility so that your questions can be answered, and you can learn your way around to some extent before moving in. If that isn't possible, have a friend or relative take pictures or a movie of the common areas and your room (if that decision has been made).

Meet with the nursing home staff ahead of time (or have your family do so if you are unable) and provide them with information about your preferences for a room location and roommate. They may not be able to accommodate all of your preferences but may be able to address your needs to some extent. Ask the staff about the routine in the nursing home and what a typical day looks like, including mealtimes. Look at a weekly menu to get an idea of what food is served and the variety offered. You should think about the personal belongings that you want to take with you and discuss this with the nursing home staff. Most places can accommodate a small piece of furniture, pictures, books, a radio, TV, or similar possessions. If some of your belongings are valuable, you'll want to make arrangements for safe storage.

You should also talk to the staff about clothing needs and decide what you need to take. Don't forget to label everything and determine how your personal laundry will be done. And, don't forget to determine the nursing home's policy on visitors. Let your friends and family know when visiting hours are and encourage them to come often.

Once you are admitted to the nursing home, it will be beneficial to you if you make an effort to get to know some of the other residents. They've all been through their own relocation experience and may be able to offer you emotional support and encouragement. One way to become acquainted with staff and residents is to participate in the activities offered at the nursing home to the extent that you are able. Group participation can be fun and help you feel more a part of your new home.

Summary

The decision to relocate to a nursing home is often a difficult one. It is more difficult when made during a crisis. It makes good sense to pay attention to your ability to live independently and to think about a time when perhaps you will not be able to remain in the community. You'll feel more in control of the situation if you've toured a few local nursing homes in anticipation of needing this level of care for yourself or someone you care about. This is not a time to be shy. Ask lots of questions and make sure you feel good about a facility before considering it as a place to live. You may never need to live in a nursing home. On the other hand, you may need a nursing home for rehabilitation or for long-term care on a more permanent basis. You'll be better equipped to handle this kind of move if you have investigated your options.

References

Some information in this chapter was adapted from the following sources.

Hunt, M. E., & Gunter-Hunt, G. (1983). Simulated site visits in the relocation of older people. *Health and Social Work*, *8*, 5–14.

Meuer, T., & Abramson, B. (1986). *A family's guide to selecting, financing and asserting rights in a nursing home.* Madison, WI: Center for Public Representation, Inc.

National Citizens' for Nursing Home Reform. (1991). *Nursing home reform law: The basics.* Washington, DC: Author.

Chapter 12

Transportation Issues to Consider

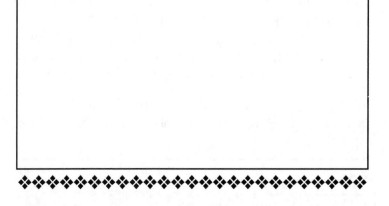

We all value our independence and mobility. We want to be able to go places whenever we want. For many years you may not have thought much about the importance of your mobility. You probably did your shopping at times that were convenient for you, planned social outings, and took trips without much planning for how you would get to these places. This chapter focuses on transportation and travel issues that you may need to consider as you grow older.

Driving

Americans are said to be in love with their automobiles. Most people in this country learn to drive when they are young and continue to drive for many years. Driving is viewed as a "right" by many people and is essential to maintaining certain lifestyles. The ability to drive also gives the person a certain status throughout life. And, of course, a driver's license is often an essential piece of identification.

Unfortunately, some people continue to drive when they no longer possess the skills needed to drive safely, such as adequate vision, good judgment, the ability to physically navigate a motor vehicle, and the ability to observe and respond to road signs and hazards. It may be difficult for a person with declining abilities to recognize that he or she could be a driving risk. In fact, a person with dementia may be unable to understand the problem entirely. Family members and/or health care providers may need to take steps to restrict a person's driving if this becomes an issue.

Transportation is essential to maintaining an independent lifestyle. You need to be able to shop for groceries and other essentials and to keep medical appointments. Likewise, you probably want to participate in social outings that are important to you and run errands when necessary. It is definitely more convenient to have your own vehicle and drive yourself these places as you need to. However, if this is not possible, many communities have other resources that can help older and disabled people with their transportation needs.

Driving Competence

Your ability to drive in all situations may change as you age. This may be because of medical or mental problems or your confidence in yourself as a driver. Older people tend to drive less as they age. Often, they feel uncomfortable driving during rush hour or at night. Likewise, some older people may be apprehensive about highway driving and less willing to take car trips. Older people who live in rural areas may feel uncomfortable driving in cities where there is more traffic and the pace is hectic. Older drivers may compensate for these concerns by driving shorter distances, avoiding night driving and rush hour, and driving generally at slower speeds. The reasons you may experience driving problems as you age are outlined below.

Physical Changes with Aging

1. *Functional problems.* As you age you may experience a decrease in your functional ability to accomplish certain tasks. You may find that you don't have the range of motion in your joints that you once had. It may be harder

for you to turn your head to look behind you or to the side of the car. You may not have the strength in your arms, hands, or legs needed to drive a stick shift or navigate with regular steering. Consequently, you may need special adaptations to your vehicle that make it easier for you to drive. The yellow pages of the phone book list companies that can adapt your vehicle. Look under *Automobile Hand and Foot Controls or Handicapped Equipment—Sales and Service.*

2. *Vision problems.* As you age, your visual acuity or ability to see sharply or clearly, decreases. Consequently, you may need prescription glasses to compensate for this loss. Older people also more frequently have diseases that cause visual impairment, such as macular degeneration (condition where the retina deteriorates) and cataracts (a clouding of the lens of the eye). Sometimes it is not possible to compensate for the loss caused by these conditions. Also, as you become older you may have difficulty with nighttime driving because of the glare problem and a decreased ability to see low contrast objects at night.

3. *Hearing problems.* This is the most common sensory loss associated with aging. Loss of hearing means that you have to pay closer attention to visual cues when driving. The risk is that you will not be able to hear warnings from emergency vehicles or other drivers that may prevent an accident.

Diseases That Impair Driving

1. *Cardiovascular (heart) disease.* If you suffer from frequent chest pain or have recently experienced a heart

attack, your physician may recommend that you not drive.

2. *Cerebral vascular accident or stroke.* If you have experienced a stroke, you may be limited physically or mentally in your ability to drive. Your state may require you to be road tested before you can drive again. Your physician also may have to submit information to the state Department of Transportation (or similar state agency that handles licensing of drivers) regarding your ability to resume safe driving. You may need a specially equipped vehicle if the stroke left you with limitations in your arms and/or legs.

3. *Alzheimer's disease or other dementia.* Dementia is a disorder characterized by memory loss, impaired judgment, and personality change. If you are diagnosed with this disorder, your ability to drive should be reviewed by your physician and by the Department of Transportation in your state. Some experts recommend that anyone with the diagnosis of dementia not drive because of decreased cognitive abilities, judgment difficulties, and other physical impairments that often are present because of this disease. One problem is that often the person with dementia lacks the ability to recognize his or her decreased abilities. Family members usually recognize the problem first and need to take steps to deal with the issue before the person with dementia has an accident. The initial step is to encourage the person to stop driving. Some individuals are willing to discontinue driving at the request of family members or a physician. However, if the person will not stop driving voluntarily, the Department of Transportation should be contacted to review the person's license.

Family members sometimes take decisive action themselves by disabling the person's vehicle.

4. *Other neurological diseases (diseases of the nervous system)*. If you are diagnosed with a neurological disease that causes problems with your ability to think, loss of consciousness, or tremors, then your ability to drive should be reviewed by the state Department of Transportation. You should submit medical information so that a decision about your driving ability can be made.

5. *Medications*. The use of prescription and over the counter medications may relate to the ability of a person to drive safely. You should always read the label or talk with your physician or pharmacist before taking a medication and driving. Some medications cause drowsiness and may slow your reaction time in an emergency. Don't forget that alcohol is a drug and a serious threat to safe driving. Mixing alcohol and medications can be even more dangerous. You should always ask your physician about any possible interactions between the medications you take and alcohol. Many people use a "designated" driver when they drink alcohol while on social outings. This person agrees not to drink alcohol and to drive everyone else who does drink home.

Driver's Retesting

The Department of Transportation (or other driver's licensing agency depending on the state in which you live) can be contacted by a physician, a relative, or other concerned party if there is concern about your ability to drive. This state agency will require that you submit medical information so that a determination can be made regarding the need to retest your driving skills. If this information indicates that there is a need for retesting, then an examination will be scheduled that will probably include both a written test and driving test.

If you or your relatives want to have your driving skills assessed, you may be able to obtain a driving skills evaluation at a local hospital or clinic. If your hospital/clinic does not offer this service, perhaps you can be referred to the closest facility that does. Driving evaluations usually are offered through the occupational therapy department. The evaluator will be examining the following abilities of the driver:

1. the ability to recognize colors, for example, red, green, and yellow;

2. the reaction time the person needs in simple and complex situations;

3. the extent of the person's visual field, including peripheral vision;

4. depth perception;

5. glare response time;

6. night vision;

7. cervical (neck) rotation;

8. arm/hand and leg function.

Often, the evaluator will test the person in an automobile simulator. This machine simulates driving on a street or highway and introduces situations to which the driver must react. Some evaluators actually ride with the person in an automobile for a driving test.

For people who feel that they can be retrained to drive a vehicle, driver's training programs are available. You may be appropriate for one of these programs if you have suffered some kind of acute event, such as a stroke, and think you can drive again with a specially equipped vehicle and retraining. Contact the Rehabilitation Department or Occupational Therapy Department at a hospital or rehabilitation center to inquire about these programs. Often university-affiliated hospitals and Department of Veterans Affairs hospitals (VA hospitals) are good resources to contact.

Loss of a Driver's License

If your driver's license is revoked by the authorities, you initially may feel angry and sad. After all, you've probably been driving for many years, and your life will change now. If your spouse can drive, the roles in your marriage will probably change. If you live alone or your spouse depended on you for driving, then your lifestyle will change more significantly. Your outings will need to be scheduled ahead of time, and you will need to allow more time to get where you are going. You'll still be able to do the things you need to do, but you'll have to be more creative when you organize outings. You may find friends or family members who are willing to transport you, or you may find a person who wants to earn extra money by providing you with rides. On the other hand, you may feel more independent by arranging your own rides using available community services. If you find that you are not able to recover from the anger or sadness you feel from losing your license, then you may need counseling with a professional social worker or psychologist to help you adjust to this loss. Your physician can probably refer you to someone who can help you cope with this important change in your life.

One way you can compensate for the loss of your license is to use available transportation resources in your community. These resources are discussed in the next section of this chapter.

Transportation Resources

Mass Transit

If you're not disabled, you may want to use the public transportation available in your area. For most cities, buses are most often used for mass transit. Larger cities may have subways or trains. If you want to use public transportation, you should contact the transit authority in your area to obtain maps of the routes and to ask any questions that you may have. You will want to know: (1) where the bus stops are located, (2) what the time schedule is for the buses, and (3) the cost of the ride. You should also inquire as to whether exact change is needed for the fare (See the picture on page 182).

Convenience of Mass Transit.

Transit for Handicapped People

Most cities provide some kind of special bus or van for individuals who because of illness or handicapped status are not able to use the regular city buses. Typically a physician must certify that the person is not able to use the regular buses due to his or her physical condition. This kind of service provides door-to-door transport with vehicles that are specially equipped to meet the needs of handicapped individuals.

In some communities, private companies offer more specialized transport for elderly and handicapped people. This kind of transportation provides a driver who will deliver a person to an exact location inside a building. For example, this service would pick you up at your hospital room and deliver you to your apartment living room using a wheel chair if necessary. Since this service is privately financed, the cost is usually more than the minimal cost of the city handicapped service but less than the cost of an ambulance. Some companies charge a base fee plus a certain monetary amount per mile. Look in the yellow pages of the phone book under *Transportation Service for Disabled* to locate the resources in your area.

Rides Programs

Some communities have local rides programs for people who need transportation to medical appointments or other necessary services. These programs are often funded through the Department of Social Services or perhaps the local Commission on Aging. The cost of these rides is reasonable and there may be community funding to help those who cannot afford the ride.

The American Cancer Society also offers the "Road to Recovery" program in some areas for cancer patients who need rides to medical appointments and are without other means of transportation. There is no charge for this service. For more information, contact your local American Cancer Society.

The Retired Senior Volunteers Program (RSVP) is a well known organization that has a network of volunteers who can help provide rides for elderly or handicapped people who are unable to procure other means of transportation. RSVP requests a donation (based on your ability to pay) to help cover the cost of the ride.

Handicapped Parking Permits

You may be eligible for a handicapped parking permit in your state if you are unable to walk past a certain distance, if you need the aid of a device to assist your walking, or if you have a medical condition that would impair your ability to walk. If you no longer drive, you can use the permit when you are a passenger in a motor vehicle. You should contact your state Department of Transportation or the Secretary of State to request an application. Your physician will need to certify your need for the permit. Most states charge a minimal fee for the permit.

Planning for Travel

You may have plans to travel when you retire. If your health is good, there is no reason to think you will not be able to travel whenever you want. You will need to be prepared for the travel snags that all travelers must face such as bad weather, flight delays, and car breakdowns. Likewise, you probably will want to consider your age and how easily you fatigue when planning your itinerary.

You may want to limit the number of hours that you travel in any one day, and you may want to plan sightseeing excursions accordingly as well. However, if you have health problems or disabilities, you'll need to plan your trips in more detail. You'll want to determine if the airlines, trains, buses, and hotels can accommodate your special needs. You might want to consider contacting a travel agent to advise you on these travel matters and to help make necessary arrangements for you.

Airlines

The major airlines and many small carriers can accommodate handicapped people with advance notice. The airlines can arrange for you to be transported by wheelchair or special vehicle from gate to gate or to a different terminal within the airport if necessary. People with special needs are allowed to board the aircraft first so that you can settle into your seat and not wait in line to get on board. A travel agent can help you make these arrangements or you can contact the airline company directly.

Trains

Amtrak can accommodate people using wheelchairs at some cities where wheelchair lifts are available. Forty-eight hours advance notice is required. Amtrak also has a special program available to all passengers that you may want to consider. The "Meet and Assist" program provides for an Amtrak employee to meet you at your train and help you to make a connection. In a large train station, this program could be helpful to you even if you are able bodied. A travel agent can help you with these arrangements or an Amtrak agent can assist you when you make your reservations.

Buses

The major bus carriers can accommodate handicapped passengers with advance notice.

Hotels

Most hotels offer "handicapped accessible" rooms with advance notice. However, the accommodations in these rooms vary greatly. When you make reservations, ask about the accessibility of the hotel's handicapped rooms to determine if your needs can be met.

Other Resources for Travel

The following resources may be helpful to you as you plan a trip.

Travel Resources

Dialysis Travel Service
9301 E. Shea Blvd. #128
Scottsdale, AZ 85260
1-800-832-5545

Travelin' Talk Network
P. O. Box 3534
Clarksville, TN 37043-3534
(615) 552-6670
(Members share knowledge of their hometowns. A quarterly newsletter includes travel tips and member information).

The Office of Tourism in individual states is also a resource to help you obtain information regarding accessibility of popular tourist attractions.

Publications

"Access Travel: Airports." (1991). A brochure describing the accessibility of terminals is published by the Airport Operators Council International and is available from the Consumer Information Center, P.O. Box 100, Pueblo, CO 81009.

Access to the World, a book edited by Louise Weiss and published in 1986 by Henry Holt & Co., (521 Fifth Avenue, New York, NY 10175) provides information regarding travel by airplane, bus, train, ship, and car. It also has a state-by-state list of access guides available for major cities and guidebooks for individual countries if you are considering travel abroad.

Twins Peaks Press publishes the following guidebooks for people with disabilities:

Directory of Travel Agencies for the Disabled (lists travel agencies around the world that specialize in travel for persons with disabilities)

Wheelchair Vagabond (tips for disabled campers)

The Disability Bookshop Catalog (books about travel and other topics of interest).

For more information on these guidebooks, call (206) 694-2462.

The Eastern Paralyzed Veterans Association provides information on travel, including a pamphlet "Ten Questions and Answers." For more information, contact EPVA at: 75-20 Astoria Blvd, Jackson Heights, NY 11370 or call 1 (800) 444-0120.

Summary

Your transportation needs and abilities may change as you age. However, resources are available that can address some of your travel needs in many locations. Local resources may be able to help you meet your basic needs, and major transportation carriers usually can accommodate passengers with special needs to some extent. As you age, you may need to become more creative when you make travel plans. However, in most cases, there is no reason to discontinue traveling if it is something you really enjoy.

Chapter 13

Legal and Financial Decision Making

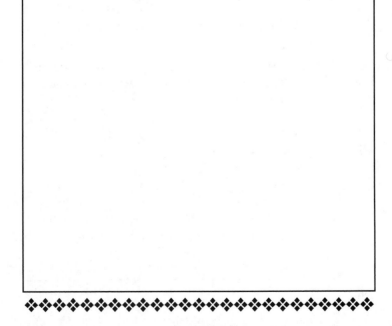

The time may come when help is needed managing finances or legal affairs. Because a crisis is never a good time to make such arrangements, some thought should be given to advance planning for maintenance of income as well as banking and legal matters. It is important to understand public benefit programs so that you can determine what you may be entitled to receive. Advance planning for financial and legal matters should focus on the least restrictive arrangements that will meet your needs. Then, you can make changes as the situation warrants. In this way, your autonomy is preserved for as long as possible.

Benefit Programs

You may be eligible for income benefits or health care benefits through federal or state programs. Because the programs providing state assistance will vary in each state, you should contact your local Department of Social Services or Commission on Aging to determine if you meet criteria in your state for assistance. Some of the benefit programs available to older people are discussed below. Your state may have other programs designed to provide assistance to older people.

Financial Benefits

Social Security

This is a federally funded benefit program for workers, retired workers, and survivors. It provides monthly cash benefits to those who meet certain qualifications. To receive benefits, you must achieve "insured status" by working a certain minimum number of quarters in employment covered by the Social Security program. Most employment (but not all) is covered by the Social Security law. If you are unsure if your employment was covered, you may request information from the Social Security Administration regarding the number of quarters recorded in your record. You must not only meet criteria in terms of coverage, but also in terms of your status as a worker. Benefits can be paid to: (1) retired workers (age 62 and over); (2) disabled workers (as defined by the Social Security Administration), (3) your dependents in certain circumstances if you are a retired or disabled worker; and (4) certain survivors after your death. You should contact the Social Security Administration for more specific information on the Social Security program and how to apply for benefits. Check the phone book federal government listings under Social Security Administration for the address and telephone number of your local office.

Supplemental Security Income(SSI)

SSI is a federal cash benefit program that is operated by the Social Security Administration. Monthly checks are provided to persons who are aged, blind and/or disabled and who meet eligibility requirements regarding financial need. In other words, the person's income is low and resources are limited. Persons who receive SSI are automatically eligible for Medical Assistance (MA). MA is defined in the section below entitled "Medical Benefits." You can contact the Social Security Administration for more information on the SSI program.

Railroad Retirement

This is a federally funded income insurance program for railroad workers. To receive a monthly benefit, you must have worked in the railroad industry for a minimum of 120 creditable months. The program is similar to Social Security in that benefits are paid for retirement and disability and for your dependents and survivors. Contact your local Railroad Retirement Board or call the Chicago office at (312) 751-4500 for more information.

Veterans Benefits

The Department of Veterans Affairs (VA) offers a variety of federally funded benefits to veterans who have been discharged from the military service and who meet VA criteria. Benefits may include financial benefits, medical benefits, educational assistance and overseas benefits. VA Hospitals are located in every state in the country and can provide medical care for eligible veterans. Some of those VA Hospitals have nursing home units for patients needing extended care. Financial benefits may be in the form of a service-connected monthly disability compensation or a nonservice-connected monthly disability pension. The service-connected compensation is awarded to veterans who were disabled by an injury or illness that was incurred in the service or which was aggravated while serving in active duty. The nonservice-connected pension is based on disability and limited income. The guidelines for VA benefits are too complex to discuss in detail in this chapter. The best way to obtain information that is current regarding VA benefits is to call the nearest VA regional office. Check the phone book federal government listings under Department of Veterans Affairs.

Each state has its own Department of Veterans Affairs that handles state benefits for the veteran population. One benefit that many states offer to eligible veterans is a retirement community setting usually called a "Veterans Home." Check the phone book state government listings for the Veterans Affairs office to determine the benefits in your state.

Medical Benefits

Medicare

This is a federally funded health insurance program for people age 65 and older and for certain disabled people. It is administered by the Health Care Financing Administration of the U.S. Department of Health and Human Services. Local Social Security offices take applications for Medicare and also provide information about the program.

There are two parts to Medicare. Hospital Insurance (Part A) helps pay for inpatient hospital care, inpatient care in a skilled nursing home (under specific conditions where skilled care is required), home health care, and hospice care. There are deductibles and co-insurance payments for Part A but most people do not have to pay a premium for the coverage. Medicare Medical Insurance (Part B) helps pay for doctor's services, outpatient hospital services, durable medical equipment, and certain other medical services and supplies that are not covered by Part A. Part B has premiums, deductibles, and co-insurance amounts that you must pay yourself or through a supplemental insurance plan.

If you are already receiving Social Security or Railroad Retirement benefit payments when you become age 65, you will automatically receive a Medicare card in the mail. You may reject Part B at that time if you so choose. You should think through this decision carefully because you may be charged a penalty if you want to add Part B at a later date. Medicare coverage is too complex to cover adequately in this chapter. If you have questions about Medicare or Social Security benefits, you can contact your local Social Security office or call the toll free telephone number 1-800-772-1213 between 7 a.m. and 7 p.m. weekdays (Eastern time).

Medical Assistance (MA), Medicaid or Title 19

MA is a joint federal-state health assistance program for certain needy and low income people. The program is administered by individual states within federal guidelines and, therefore, varies somewhat from state to state in terms of benefits and eligibility criteria. Medical Assistance is a companion program to the Supplemental Security Income (SSI) and the Aid to Families with Dependent Children (AFDC) programs. SSI and AFDC recipients are automatically eligible for Medical Assistance. If you're in a nursing home and your income is less than the amount set by state law, you would qualify for coverage (see Nursing Homes, Chapter 11). If you don't qualify for Medical Assistance because your income is over the limit, you may still qualify as medically needy. In this situation, your medical expenses are considered when your income is calculated. If you are eligible for Medical Assistance, you will need to receive your health care from a physician who participates in the Medical Assistance program. Basic services are mandated by federal law. However, the total coverage provided by MA depends on each state's program.

Veterans Health Care

The Department of Veterans Affairs offers medical benefits to eligible veterans. Hospital or outpatient care is provided to treat all service-connected disabilities at a VA hospital, clinic, or, under restricted circumstances, at the office of a local provider. Service-connected disabilities are those disabilities rated by the VA as related to a person's active duty. Hospital or outpatient care also is available to other groups of veterans on a space available basis based on certain criteria determined by the Department of Veterans Affairs. In some instances the VA may also provide or pay for nursing home care, usually on a time limited basis. The best way to determine your eligibility for medical benefits at a VA Hospital is to contact the eligibility clerk at your local VA hospital. Be prepared to provide certain documentation of your military service, such as your discharge papers.

Practical Suggestions for Your Medical Bills

Medical bills can sometimes be confusing and overwhelming. You may not be familiar with the codes used on the bill or the names of procedures or medications administered in the hospital or at the physician's office. Even so, you should consider yourself to be a consumer of health care just as when you make any other major purchase.

The following strategies can help you "keep tabs" on your medical bills.

1. Obtain information about procedures and tests that your physician recommends. Find out what your insurance company considers to be a "reasonable and customary" charge for that procedure and discuss this with your physician.

2. Review your bills and the explanation of benefits (or e.o.b.) forms that you receive from your insurer. If you find an error or do not understand a particular charge, call the billing office of the provider (physician or hospital) for clarification. If you have difficulty understanding the bill, request that the billing office staff explain the bill to you. A social worker or county benefits specialist is another resource if you feel you need an advocate to help you interact with Medicare or a local hospital or physician's office.

3. Keep track of the deductibles you need to pay before your insurance covers a service. If you have family coverage, you may meet your deductible sooner than if you have individual coverage.

4. If your insurance coverage is not adequate to cover your bills or if you don't have insurance, don't panic. Most providers (hospitals, clinics, or doctor's offices) are

willing to schedule a monthly payment arrangement that you can afford. You might also consider asking for a referral to a social worker who can determine if you are eligible for any financial assistance programs.

5. If you are currently employed and considering retirement, check out the insurance coverage your employer offers to retirees. If you are anticipating sizable medical bills soon, you might want to delay your retirement.

Prior to retirement, you will want to know how long you can continue coverage under the company health plan and how the plan is coordinated with Medicare. If your employer's group retirement plan is costly, you may want to investigate the cost and coverage of other Medicare supplemental policies. A free booklet, *Consumer's Guide to Medical Supplemental Insurance*, can help you. It is available from the Health Insurance Association of America, Box 41455, Washington, DC 20018.

Banking

A joint bank account commonly is used by married couples and by other persons sharing funds. A joint bank account allows you and the other party to individually withdraw funds at will and make deposits as well. It is simple to open and use. Either party can use the account without permission of the other person. This type of account can be a problem, however, if a person with impaired judgment withdraws funds without understanding what he or she is doing. A cognitively impaired person may be taken advantage of by others wishing to defraud him or her. One way to protect an account from this type of abuse is to arrange a dual-signature account. In this arrangement, both persons must sign for withdrawals. This simple alternative must be arranged while both parties are competent and the services of an attorney are not necessary. The bank can make the arrangements to change the account by having the necessary forms completed by the account holders. One caution regarding this type of account is that it should not be used unless the money in the account belongs to both parties. This is important because the money appears to the bank to belong to both signers. The risk for abuse exists in that the more competent person could persuade the other person to sign over the account. Another complication is that special arrangements must be made if one of the co-signers dies. Check with the bank that you use to determine the procedure to be used to withdraw funds if one party dies.

Durable Power of Attorney: Financial Matters

A "power of attorney" is a written legal document that grants you, the principal, the authority to appoint another person to make certain decisions for you. The power of attorney may be limited to specific situations or be limited to authority over specific accounts or resources. Or, a power of attorney may give broad authority to act on the principal's behalf. Traditionally, a power of attorney was void when a person became incapacitated. At that point, families had to seek financial guardianship to manage the affairs of a relative. These proceedings could be expensive and cumbersome. Fortunately, most states have now enacted the "durable power of attorney" which permits you to appoint someone whose authority to make these decisions can continue even after you, the principal, are incapacitated.

The durable power of attorney can be a valuable document for a caregiver who may need to make important financial decisions and transactions to properly provide care for a person. It allows these kinds of decisions to be made promptly and it avoids the cost of initiating a guardianship (legal proceeding whereby someone is appointed to make decisions for an incapacitated person). It is important to note that a competent person can cancel his or her power of attorney at any time.

Advance Directives for Health Care Decisions

An advance directive is a document that allows you to state your wishes regarding health care treatment prior to a time of incapacity. As long as you retain decision-making capacity, your health care providers will continue to consult with you regarding your treatment. If you become incapacitated, however, you may not be able to discuss these matters with your health care providers. An advance directive allows that communication with an agent you select ahead of time if your own decision-making capacity is lost. Two types of advance directives are discussed below: the Durable Power of Attorney for Health Care and the Living Will.

Durable Power of Attorney for Health Care

In this document, you (the principal) appoint another person (the health care agent) to make health care decisions for you if you are no longer capable of making your own decisions. It is important for you to discuss with your agent such issues as resuscitation, life-support procedures, organ donations, organ transplants, autopsies, and preferences for health care providers and facilities to be used. You should choose an agent that you trust to carry out your wishes. It is a good idea to discuss your Durable Power of Attorney for Health Care with your physician, and once it is completed a copy should be placed in the medical record in your physician's office or clinic.

You can find out if the Durable Power of Attorney for Health Care is an option in your state by contacting the State Department of Health and Social Services, the office of the state Attorney General, or a local Commission on Aging. These agencies should be able to help you obtain a copy of the document if it is legal in your state.

Living Will

A Living Will is a document you can complete to inform your physician that you do not wish the dying process to be prolonged by artificial means if illness or injury is incurable. Living Will laws in some states may restrict its use to when a terminal illness is present. Some Living Will statutes allow for the designation of a proxy to make decisions for you if you are not able to do so yourself. It is important to make sure that close family members and your health care providers have a copy of your Living

Will. You should also find out if a photocopy of a completed Living Will is valid in your state. If not, you will need to complete the desired number of original documents for family and health care providers. Your Living Will can be revoked according to the laws in your state. Typically, you can tear up the document, verbally revoke it, or revoke it in writing. A written revocation that you provide to each person who was given a copy of the Living Will document is the best means of revoking it.

As with the Durable Power of Attorney for Health Care, check with the State Department of Health and Social Services, the office of the state Attorney General, or the local Commission on Aging to determine if the Living Will is valid in your state. These agencies also can help you obtain a copy of the document if it is legal in your state.

Living Will or Durable Power of Attorney for Health Care: Which is Best?

Of course, you will have to make your own decision regarding the use of an advance directive. However, some of the points mentioned in this section may make your decision a little easier.

A Durable Power of Attorney for Health Care that allows you to state your specific desires and specify special provisions or limitations regarding your health care can do everything that a Living Will can do, and more. The Durable Power of Attorney for Health Care has the benefit of providing for an agent who can remind the doctor or medical team of your wishes and take necessary measures to make sure your wishes are being respected. Overall, the Durable Power of Attorney for Health Care provides broader coverage regarding health care decisions than most Living Will documents. With the Durable Power of Attorney for Health Care, you do not need to foresee every possible kind of medical situation because you have chosen someone who can discuss each situation with the health care team as the need arises.

However, this document may not be an option in all states. And, if you do not know anyone willing to be your agent, you will not be able to complete a Durable Power of Attorney for Health Care document. In this instance, a Living Will or some other kind of health care treatment directive will suit your needs better.

It is to your advantage to find out what the law is in your state regarding advance directives. Only then can you make an informed decision that will address your needs. You can receive free information on advance directives from Choice in Dying, 200 Varick Street, New York, NY 10014 (212-366-5540).

Conservatorship

This arrangement is similar to a guardianship of the estate. However, conservatorship is voluntary whereas guardianship is involuntary. You must be competent to seek a conservatorship, and then you nominate someone to take charge of your financial matters. Typically, people seeking conservatorship are physically disabled and often overwhelmed with managing their affairs. In many situations, conservatorship has been replaced with the Durable Power of Attorney.

However, some people may view the accountability to the court as an advantage of the conservatorship. Also, a conservatorship allows you to exercise some control over your property if the conservator and the court do not object, for example, making gifts to others. The disadvantages of a conservatorship include the expense of setting it up and interacting with the court for certain matters, including termination of the conservatorship if so desired.

Payee Arrangements

This is another mechanism for handling financial affairs in which a person is appointed to receive Social Security, Supplemental Security Income, or Department of Veterans Affairs payments for another person. A payeeship may be voluntary or imposed on you if you are unable to manage your funds. The payee is obligated to use your funds to provide support for you and must report to the agency providing the benefits. Social Security calls this person a representative payee, and the Department of Veterans Affairs calls this person a fiduciary. Both agencies have broad powers in this area and can appoint a payee when doing so is seen as being in the best interests of the beneficiary. This can be the case even if you are considered legally competent. Documentation from a physician regarding your ability to manage your funds is required by both agencies when a payee arrangement is considered. The advantage of this type of arrangement is that court proceedings are avoided.

Guardianship

The time may come when you are no longer able to make decisions about financial matters or decisions about your personal welfare. This change could occur quite suddenly as a result of an accident or abrupt illness. On the other hand, this change could occur over many years as a result of Alzheimer's disease or some other illness that affects memory and judgment. Typically, family members notice the change in ability to function and seek medical help. If a physician determines that you are unable to make decisions for yourself, then the recommendation will be that your family or significant others consider legal measures to protect you as an incapacitated person.

The best time to plan for this kind of problem is well before it happens. Some of the legal documents already mentioned can address this issue. For example, the Durable Power of Attorney can provide coverage for financial matters when you can no longer make financial decisions on your own, and the Durable Power of Attorney for Health Care can provide coverage for health care decisions if you can no longer make these decisions. If these mechanisms can adequately be used, guardianship may be avoided. However, if these alternatives are not in place at the time you become incapacitated or in situations where a protective placement is needed, guardianship can be a valuable legal resource.

A guardianship is the appointment by the court of a person to make decisions for an incapacitated person. These decisions relate either to property or personal care. For the court to order a guardianship for you, there must be a finding of incompetence. In other words, you must be substantially incapable of caring for yourself or managing property. Incompetence is based on your inability to care for yourself, not your unwillingness to do so.

Types of Guardianships

The laws on guardianship may vary somewhat from state to state. This section discusses the basic types of guardianship. You may want to check with an attorney in your state to see how your law is written.

Temporary Guardianship

A *temporary guardianship* is limited to a finite number of days and allows the court to appoint a guardian in situations where the welfare of a person who is currently incompetent requires immediate attention. For example, you might need a temporary guardianship in situations where extreme depression or malnutrition is interfering with your ability to care for yourself. The primary goal of the guardianship is usually to obtain services or needed medical attention for you and then to determine if a full guardianship is needed.

Limited Guardianship

A *limited guardianship* occurs when the court finds that you are impaired but can still control some aspects of your life. The limited guardian has certain specific duties with the impaired person remaining in charge of all other legal matters; a limited guardian may be either of the person or property.

Full Guardianship

A *full guardianship* occurs when you (as an impaired person) are found to be incompetent by the court. The court-appointed guardian has complete charge of decisions related to you. Guardianship of the person means that you can no longer make decisions about your health or other daily needs. Guardianship of the property means that you can no longer make decisions about managing your money or financial matters. The court may appoint either a full guardian of your person, property, or both.

Duties of a Guardian

A guardian is given the responsibility by the court for the care of the incompetent person, and that person is said to be in the custody and control of the guardian. Of course, guardianships are administered in different ways but there are basic responsibilities the guardian must accept. Generally the duties of a guardian of the person are:

1. To meet the basic needs of the person (or ward); (this means that the guardian must make sure that the impaired person has adequate food, clothing, shelter, and medical care. The guardian does not necessarily

have to provide for these needs personally, but must make arrangements to meet these needs.)

2. To assure that the rights and best interests of the incompetent person are preserved;

3. To provide informed consent for medical procedures;

4. To report to the court, according to state law;

5. To arrange for community services.

The duties of a guardian of the property are:

1. To manage the finances and assets of the person;

2. To pay bills for the person;

3. To apply for financial assistance and government benefits as appropriate.

Authority of a Guardian

There are limits to the authority of a guardian. These limitations may vary from state to state. Some examples of limitations are:

1. Protective placement. A guardian may not be able to place a ward in an institution or nursing home except on a very short-term basis. A petition must be filed with the court for such placement.

2. Transfer of real estate. This type of transaction requires a petition from the guardian to the court in most situations.

3. Autopsy. A guardian may not object to the deceased person's family providing consent for an autopsy.

4. Anatomical gifts. Under certain circumstances, a guardian may make a gift of body parts when a ward dies. These circumstances may vary from state to state.

Protective Placement

The day may come when, because of disability or incapacity, you cannot continue to live independently or be cared for in the community. Your care needs may become so great that it is not possible financially or emotionally for those coordinating your care to continue to do so in the home. If you are not competent to make your own decisions about your living situation and you are considered to be at risk of harming yourself or others, then guardianship and protective placement into a more suitable living environment will need to be arranged. Typically, family members or significant others initiate these proceedings through the court.

If guardianship proceedings are initiated for you, you are entitled to legal representation and to have a guardian ad litem appointed to ensure your best interests. A *guardian ad litem* is an attorney appointed by the court to serve as your advocate during the court proceedings. The Department of Social Services or whichever state agency is responsible for protective placements must also ensure that you have been evaluated regarding the need for protective placement. The results of this evaluation will be provided to the court. The goal of this agency is to recommend the least restrictive environment for placement. For example, some people can be protectively placed in a group home as opposed to a nursing home. If the court decides in favor of guardianship and protective placement, arrangements will be made for your status to be reviewed periodically. It is also the responsibility of the guardian to make sure that you are receiving good care. Of course, the specific laws governing protective placement will vary somewhat from state to state.

Wills

A will is a means for you to dispose of certain types of your property after your death. Most of you have probably thought about what you want to happen to your property, but unless you have a will, you cannot be sure that your wishes will be honored. Each state has laws governing the distribution of property if a person dies without a will. The court that has jurisdiction over the administration of the estates of deceased persons is called probate court. Property will pass to survivors through certain property laws. Some property, called nonprobate property, is not subject to laws of the probate court. For example, property owned in joint tenancy with someone else is considered nonprobate and is not subject to the terms of a will. If you want to control dispersal of your property, you should strongly consider writing a will. The first step is for you to determine what property you have that is subject to the laws of the probate court and decide how you want to distribute it. In some states, you can write your own basic will. There may even be a simple form that you can obtain and complete. A public advocacy law firm or a state Area Office on Aging may be able to help you locate such a form. This kind of will may not fit your needs if your property holdings are complex or if you have children from a previous marriage that you want to name in your will. It may also not be appropriate if you own business property. If a basic will does not work for you, then you should consider consulting an attorney to help draft your will. When writing a will, you should be very specific in terms of naming possessions that you want left to certain people. This will help avoid family arguments as to who was promised what property or prized possessions.

Trusts

Testamentary Trust

You may want to consider a trust as part of your will. A trust is an arrangement where you direct that, at your death, someone (a trustee) will handle certain assets for the benefit of beneficiaries that you have named. Your trustee will distribute the income or the principal from the trust in the manner set forth in your will. A financial institution can be named to manage a trust, typically when a large estate is involved. Trusts can be used when property is left to minor children or when it is a goal to reduce inheritance or income taxes. A trust can also be used if the beneficiaries are not viewed by the person with the property as being capable of handling the estate or if management of the estate is burdensome. If you are arranging a trust, you should consult an attorney and/or a trust officer at your local bank.

Living Trust

A living trust or revocable living trust is a trust created during a person's lifetime that can be amended or terminated at any time. In this arrangement, the person setting up the trust transfers ownership of assets to a trustee (a bank, trust company or an individual) whose responsibility is to hold and manage the funds for a beneficiary. The person setting up the trust, the trustee and the beneficiary may all be the same person or different people may be involved. The trustee manages the funds and keeps accurate records of all transactions

Living trusts can be created earlier than actually needed whereby you manage your funds as long as you are able and then, at the occurrence of a particular event, management of the trust shifts to your trustee. This "stand-by trust" can be set up to go into effect if you become physically or mentally incapacitated.

A living trust can also be used to distribute assets after death. You can design your estate plan so that your retirement benefits, life insurance proceeds, and other benefits are payable to the trustee of your living trust to be managed under the terms of the trust. Your will also can provide for your estate assets to be placed into the trust to be administered under the trust's provisions.

One important consideration regarding a trust is that it can affect your tax situation, your estate plan, and even your eligibility for Medical Assistance. *Therefore, you should always consult an attorney before establishing a living trust.* If you are interested in a living trust, you should contact your local bank to determine any requirements established by that institution. You should also inquire regarding the cost of arranging and maintaining the trust.

An attorney can advise you as to whether you should consider a living trust. In some states, where the probate laws are informal, such an arrangement may be unnecessary for the person with a smaller estate. You should check out the reliability of companies selling living trusts or do-it-yourself living trust kits. Fraud has been reported in this area. Estate planning is a task that takes time and expertise. Therefore, you should carefully consider trust arrangements and not make on-the-spot or hasty decisions that may not be in your best interest.

Summary

Legal decision making is extremely important for all adults. The best time to make decisions about managing your finances or legal affairs is before a crisis. If you make these kinds of arrangements ahead of time, your family or significant others have the authority they may need to help manage your affairs if you are not able to do so yourself.

It is never pleasant to think about incapacity, but all adults should do so for the sake of those who care about them. You also will be able to protect more of your estate by using advance planning alternatives that avoid guardianship proceedings, such as the Durable Power of Attorney. Court proceedings can be costly and time consuming.

References

Some information in this chapter was adapted from the following sources.

Abramson, B. (1992). *Guardianship and advance planning alternatives.* Madison, WI: Center for Public Representation, Inc.

Abramson, B., & Groom, M. (1989). *Senior citizens and the law.* Madison, WI: Center for Public Representation, Inc.

Center for Public Representation, Inc. (1984). *Guardianships, conservatorships and powers of attorney.* Madison, WI: Author.

Department of Veterans Affairs. (1992). *Federal benefits for veterans and dependents.* Washington, DC: Author.

Dicks, H. M., & Abramson, B. (1990). *Planning for future health care decisions.* Madison, WI: Center for Public Representation, Inc.

Dunkin, A. (1992). Retirees, your health plans look a bit peaked. *Business Week, 3295,* 114–115.

Hepburn, K. (1989). *Working with financial and legal advisors: Guardianships and involuntary treatment.* Minneapolis, MN: GRECC.

Klug, M. J. (1985). *The basic wills handbook.* Madison, WI: Center for Public Representation, Inc.

Rowland, M. (1992, December 6). Keeping tabs on medical bills. *The New York Times,* 17.

Titunik, V. (1992, January 12). Living trust isn't suitable for everyone. *The Milwaukee Journal,* B1 and B7.

U.S. Department of Health and Human Services. (1992). *The Medicare handbook.* Baltimore, MD: Author.

Appendix

Resource Agencies and Advocacy Groups

Advocacy Groups

Coalition of Advocates for
   Rights of Infirm Elderly
   (CARIE)
1315 Walnut Street, Suite 900
Philadelphia, PA 19107
(215) 545-5728
(Telephone referral service for
   older people who are disabled
   or infirm.)

The Hastings Center
360 Broadway
Hastings-on-Hudson
New York, NY 10706
(914) 762-8500
(Issues of aging: moral issues of
   medical technology, dying,
   national health care, and
   long-term care.)

Resource Agencies

**Children and Family of Aging
   Parents**
Children of Aging Parents
2761 Trenton Road
Levittown, PA 19056
(215) 547-1070
(Provides information on housing and caregiving for children and families of seniors.
   Send self-addressed, stamped
   envelope for information.)

Communication Services
Lifeline Systems
1 (800) 451-0525
In Alaska, Hawaii, and

Massachusetts: (617) 923-4141
(Information on Lifeline
   Systems, an emergency telephone system for senior
   citizens.)

Tele-Consumer Hotline
1 (800) 332-1124
In Washington, DC:
   (202) 483-4100
(Answers questions on your telephone service and equipment
   and tells you where to go to
   find further assistance, ways
   to cut costs, and solutions to
   billing problems.)

Life Safety Systems, Inc.
2100 M Street NW, #305
Washington, DC 20037

Medic Alert
Turlock, CA 95381
1 (800) 344-3226
(For bracelets with personal
   medical information. Also,
   this organization will make
   your medical data available
   for emergency help.)

Consumer Issues
Better Business Bureaus
1515 Wilson Boulevard
Arlington, VA 33309
(703) 276-0100
(Consumer protection offering
   pamphlets on funerals, hearing
   aids, land scams, and more.)

Consumer Information Center
P.O. Box 100

Pueblo, CO 81002
(719) 948-3334
(Education and information office of the federal government. Provides free or low-cost pamphlets on a variety of topics including housing, drugs and food safety, home safety, wise buying practices, home repair, and more.)

Food and Drug Administration
5600 Fishers Lane
Rockville, MD 20856
(301) 443-3170
(This federal agency provides extensive information on food, drugs, and cosmetics.)

National Consumers League
1522 C Street NW, Suite 406
Washington, DC 20005

United Seniors Consumer
Cooperative
1334 G Street NW, Suite 500
Washington, DC 20005
(202) 393-6222
(Nonprofit organization that offers extensive health care information and low-cost services to older members nationwide. Extensive computer base tells you the best doctors, dentists, or medical specialists in your area. Analyses medi-gap insurance plans available in your state and offers a special service to remind you of annual physical or dates for medical tests.)

Education
Arthritis Service Network
Arthritis Foundation
1314 Spring Street NW
Atlanta, GA 30309
(404) 351-0454
(A health education network offering health programs on self-help and exercise nationwide. Call or write for pamphlets.)

Elderhostel
80 Boylston Street, Suite 400
Boston, MA 02116
(Provides a catalog of international schools and universities cooperating in a program of education for seniors, including living arrangements on campuses.)

National Library
Service for the Blind
1 (800) 336-4797
Alaska, Hawaii, Virginia, Washington, DC:
collect (703) 522-2590
(Operated by the Library of Congress. Call for information about reading materials and help with research.)

Health
Alcoholics Anonymous (AA)
P.O. Box 459 Grand Central Station
New York, NY 10163

Alzheimer's Disease and Related Disorders Association

70 East Lake Street, Suite 600
Chicago, IL 60601
1 (800) 621-0379
In Illinois: 1 (800) 572-6037
(Information on Alzheimer's
    disease.)

American Cancer Society
4 West 35th Street
New York, NY 10001
1 (800) 4CANCER

American Council of the Blind
1 (800) 424-8666
(Information on causes and
    treatment of blindness.)

American Diabetes Association
2 Park Avenue
New York, NY 10016
(212) 683-7444

American Heart Association
7320 Greenville Avenue
Dallas, TX 75231
(214) 750-5397
(Publications on heart disease.
    Supports research on heart
    attack, stroke, and other heart
    and blood vessel disease.)

American Lung Association
1740 Broadway
P.O. Box 596
New York, NY 10019
(212) 245-8000

American Kidney Fund
1 (800) 638-8299
In Maryland: 1 (800) 492-8361
In Washington, DC:

1 (301) 986-1444
(Information on kidney disease.)

American Osteopathic
    Association
142 E. Ontario Street
Chicago, IL 60611
(312) 208-5800
(General information about osteo-
    pathic medicine and referral
    sources to practitioners.)

Arthritis Foundation
3400 Peachtree Road, NE,
    Room 1101
Atlanta, GA 30326
(404) 351-0454
(Arthritis research: offers publi-
    cations, and operates Arthritis
    Service Network.)

The American Parkinson
    Disease Association, Inc.
60 Bay Street, Suite 401
Staten Island, NY 10301
1 (800) 223-2732

Health Care
American Health Care
    Association
1200 15th Street NW, 8th Floor
Washington, DC 20005
(202) 833-2050

American Hospital Association
840 North Lake Shore Drive
Chicago, IL 60611
(312) 280-6000

American Medical Association
535 North Dearborn Street

Chicago, IL 60611
(312) 751-6426

National Association of
Home Care
518 C Street NE
Washington, DC 20002
(202) 547-7424

National Association of Private
Geriatric Case Managers
Box 6920 Yorkville Station
New York, NY 10128
(212) 831-5582

National Association of
Rehabilitation Agencies
1700 K Street NW
Washington, DC 20009
(202) 842-0440

National Institute on
Adult Day Care
Department P, 600 Maryland
Avenue SW
West Wing 100
Washington, DC 20024

Insurance
Health Care Financing
Administration
Department of Health
and Human Services
Baltimore, MD 21207
(301) 966-3000
(Excellent publications
on Medicare.)

Legal
Commission on Legal Problems
of the Elderly

American Bar Association
1800 M Street NW
Washington, DC 20036

Legal Counsel for the Elderly
c/o AARP
1909 K Street, NW
Washington, DC 20049
(202) 234-0970
(Self-help legal information for
older people.)

National Association of State
Units on Aging
600 Maryland Avenue SW,
Suite 208, West Wing
Washington, DC 20024
(202) 484-7182
(Provides information on current
legislative and regulatory
issues and policies affecting
state aging programs.
Send for publications.)

National Senior Citizens
Law Center
2025 M Street NW, Suite 400
Washington, DC 20036

**Social Security, Pensions,
Federal Taxes, Welfare**
IRS Taxpayer Assistance
1 (800) 424-1040
(Information on problems and
questions about taxes.)

Pensions Rights Center
1701 K Street NW
Washington, DC 20006
(Publications about
pension rights.)

Social Security Hotline
1 (800) 662-1111
(Information on Social Security
benefits and federal income
taxes.)

U.S. Department of Labor
Pension and Welfare
    Benefit Programs
Office of Communications
    Room N4662
200 Constitution Avenue NW
Washington, DC 20210
(Information about the rights of
senior citizens under federal
private-pension laws.)

**Special Interest Groups for
    Seniors**
Gray Panthers
311 South Juniper Street, #601
Philadelphia, PA 19102
(215) 545-6555

National Association
    of Mature People (NAMP)
2212 NW 50th Street
P.O. Box 26792
Oklahoma, OK 73126
(405) 848-1832

National Council of
    Senior Citizens
925 15th Street NW
Washington, DC 20005
(202) 347-8800

National Rehabilitation
    Information Center
1 (800) 34NARIC

(Information about products to
make life easier for disabled
people.)

Older Women's League (OWL)
1325 G Street NW (LLB)
Washington, DC 20005

Veterans Administration
1 (800) 622-4134
(Information to veterans and
their dependents on benefits
for education, health care, disability, and retirement.)

Travel
American Society of Travel
    Agents, Inc.
4400 MacArthur Boulevard, NW
Washington, DC 20007
(202) 965-7520
(Free literature, such as: *The
United States Welcomes
Handicapped Visitors.*)

Volunteer Programs
Service Corps of Retired
    Executives
1129 Twentieth Street NW,
    Suite 410
Washington, DC 20036
(Matches the experience of
retired business people with
small businesses needing help,
on a volunteer basis.)

Volunteer Hotlines
1 (800) 424-8580
In Alaska and Hawaii:
    1 (800) 424-9704
(Information on the Peace Corps